Motivation for the 21st Century

MOTIVACT!ON FOR LIFE

7 Secrets For Living Your Dreams Now

SMILJAN MORI

MotivAction for Life

© 2013, All Rights Reserved Smiljan Mori

No part of this publication may be reproduced, stored in a retrieval system, or transmitted, in any form or by any means, electronic, mechanical, photocopying, recording or otherwise, without the prior written permission of the author. Violation of copyright will be punished to the full extent of international law.

www.SmiljanMori.com/en, info@smiljanmori.com

DISCLAIMER:

While all the techniques in this book when properly applied can have a significant and positive impact on your life, please note that this information neither constitutes medical, legal nor any other professional advice, nor replaces advice from your own accountant, attorney, or advisors. You are strongly advised to consult your medical, legal advisors for any matters that pertain your health and legal matters. The material in this book and ancillary materials that may be later provided are for educational, motivational and informational purposes only and is not intended as medical nor legal advice. Also, if you have significant physical or mental health issues, you are highly advised to consult a licensed physician at your earliest moment.

There is no guarantee, express or implied, that you will earn any money using the techniques and ideas in this book. Examples in these materials are not to be interpreted as a promise or guarantee of earnings. Earning potential is entirely dependent on the efforts and skills of the person applying all or part of the concepts, ideas and strategies contained herein.

The author, publisher and distributors cannot be held liable for the use or misuse of this information and you hereby agree to take responsibility for your use of this material. If you do not agree with these terms, please return the book.

For general information on our other products and services, please find our contact information online at www.SmiljanMori.com/en

To purchase customized or bulk copies of this book, please visit us online at www.bestsellersuccess.com/bulk

ISBN No. 978-1-922093-09-7
Cover Designer: Kathy Dunn
Publisher: Best Seller Success
Las Vegas, Nevada, USA
Ph: 702 997 2229 email: Support@BestSellerSuccess.com

www.BestSellerSuccess.com

MotivAction for Life so moved the following readers they felt motivated to remark:

MotivAction for Life is a delightful book filled with useful information to help you create a more satisfying, powerful and loving life.

Susan Jeffers, Ph.D., Author of FEEL THE FEAR AND DO IT ANYWAY

The master motivator reveals the seven secrets.
This is a fine book by an extraordinary leader.

Dan Poynter, The Self-Publishing Manual

Collected in one volume are the essential secrets to a healthy, happy and successful life. Smiljan Mori has written a handbook for living that should be required reading for every first-year college student! Use these secrets and live your best life.

Cynthia Richmond, author "Dream Power, How To Use Your Night Dreams To Change Your Life."

"*Smiljan Mori is a master of the fundamentals of success. His step by step approach makes it easy for both the novice and the serious success student to solidify the basics necessary for growth in today's fast-paced world.*"

Christopher Guerriero Author of the Best-Selling book Maximize Your Metabolism ®

"*When you first meet Smiljan Mori, you immediately notice that there is something special about him. Read his book, "MotivAction for Life",* and do all the exercises in it. Your will find that your life WILL change positively and there will be no looking back."

Veronica Lim, Founder of Millionaire Thinking, www.millionairethinking.com

"Smiljan's book isn't for everybody. It is aimed only at the smartest investors, those who decide to invest in the most profitable known asset - themselves. You will find enough advice in the book for success in private and professional life. You just have to add some will and action. Recommended."

Aleš Lisac, manager of the company Lisac & Lisac

"Proof that a man can develop, with a small amount of will and persistence, unbelievable capabilities, is available in this book. Smiljan Mori tells us in a clear, simple and sincere way that joy of life, self-confidence, success and happiness lie within ourselves, and that we can gain them very simply. It is a must-read for those who would like to make something more of their lives."

Denis Stroligo, President of Merkur Insurance Company

"We could spare ourselves a few bitter experiences in our lives if we followed the instructions in this book. This book should be among the obligatory readings at schools. Then we would put into the hands of our children a compass and a map so that they could discover the masterpiece of their own lives. But, of course, for sailing, a compass and a map aren't enough. You must also take the first step by turning "motivation" into "action." Read the book. It can change your life for the better!"

Mirko Zamernik, Major of Luče ob Savinji

"Each of us controls his life by autopilot. It is up to us alone how much we demand from ourselves and to what extent we use all our potential. This book is more proof that I'm on the right track. I will keep the altitude of my flight very high. The book MotivAction for Life I recommend to everyone who doesn't want to leave the autopilot to chance. The book will really help you to become the main actor of your own life."

Alenka Dovzan, member of the Slovenian women's A ski team and winner of an Olympic bronze medal

"I admire Smiljan as a man who has hidden an enormous amount of positive energy. His immense desire for success and a happy, fulfilled life, led him to research and try different techniques and methods of self-control and motivation. Each man is the blacksmith of his own happiness - this principle works very well for him. Here we learn about all of his rich experiences and knowledge he unselfishly shares with others. The book is an excellent manual for those who want to start to live each day at a time in a happier way."

Matej Bregant, Manager of the Slowatch company

"This book is an excellent manual for making changes in your life and to start living your dreams, instead of just dreaming about them."

Darja Herman and Dejan Cvetrežnik, who made a change in their lives and are living their dreams today

"MotivAction for Life is an excellent manual, which can help everyone who follows the offered instructions achieve significant progress in all key aspects of their lives. Smiljan Mori, the #1 motivator in Slovenia, explains in a very persuasive, sometimes even witty way, how motivation is the indispensable fuel on the road to achieving your goals. If decisions made aren't followed by action, however, there won't be results. I'm sure that there are going to be many readers who say: "This is the book that changed my life!"

Franci Kotnik, Secretary of the area Mozirje Chamber of Commerce and manager of Savinjske Novice

"Fresh and active approaches for everyone who wants to succeed and live more of life."

Franjo Trojnar, author of the book The Vision of Success

"That a book is a weapon (Brecht) is verified with Smiljan's first book, MotivAction for Life, which will be a great help for readers in planning and achieving many personal and professional victories. Encouraging and very useful!"

Uroš Skuhala, Manager, management unit Maribor, Insurance Maribor, d. d.

"Fantastic! I think this book should be obligatory for all athletes. Congratulations! Those who read it will become more MOTIV(ACTION)ED and life in general will get FASTER, HIGHER AND STRONGER. As a sports teacher and coach, I would like to thank you in the name of all who, with the help of this book, are going to achieve better results. And most of all, thanks for helping me be an incredibly positive person and a better teacher and coach!"

Marjan Pušnik, football coach CMC PUBLIKUM

"Private enterprise is one of the most demanding life challenges, mostly because it very much depends on the personality of the owner and his or her life energy and determination. If everything is in the right place in the psyche, entrepreneurial success follows, claims Smiljan, who leads us to a confrontation with ourselves, to the solving of unconscious knots, which may cause the release of creative energy. Will it be followed by business success? Not necessarily, but maybe you will find something else - your happiness."

Jože Vilfan, editor of the magazine, The Businessman

"This book is meant for everyone who would like to improve their quality of life. Smiljan Mori offers many solutions and proven instructions on how to direct your actions to achieve happiness in life. Most will be gained by those who put the offered instructions into practice."

Milan Topolovec, manager of the company, Jeruzalem Ormož SAT, D.D.

"You will achieve a goal if you really believe in it, and Smiljan Mori helps you with that perfectly in his book, MotivAction for Life. And if you are lucky enough to be at the right place at the right time, success is inevitable."

Andrej Osterc, member of the management of Insurance Merkur, d.d.

"Surely for each of us there comes a time when we start to think about ourselves and our self-image. 'Did we create anything useful in our life - positive for us and our surroundings?' Answers to this kind of question usually aren't very good, and, of course, aren't a useful factor on the way to self-improvement. The author leads you smoothly through the chapters on the way to changes in your life and self-image, no matter what your present condition. It is also important that the book isn't some kind of reading notice about something, but is rather a trigger to the process, through practical examples of how you can quickly and efficiently achieve important goals in the field of personal growth."

Peter Kavčič jr., businessman

"I read somewhere that life is determined by one of three factors: fear, courage or passion.

The one who is afraid all the time is always passive and always discontented.

The one who is very brave will do something very big - but only to prove (mostly to himself) that he isn't really afraid. And he is, at least for a time, satisfied.

The person who really wants to live life has to press those buttons which really motivate him and evoke a passion toward life. One of those buttons is Smiljan's book. Read it. If you find out that you need more, press another button. Go to one of the Smiljan seminars. In that way, you will finally press all the right buttons to play the intended melody of your life. Only you can be its composer. Don't waste the opportunity! I myself pressed both. Come and ask me how I am - now..."

Mojca Poljanšek, editor of the magazine, Rina

ACKNOWLEDGMENTS

First, I thank my great love Helena. Thank you for teaching me sincere and honest love and thank you for waking me up with your beautiful smile. Thank you also for all the energy, love and support you give so generously. Without you, I could not have become who I am. I adore you. Praise also to Ivan and Milena Kodrič who have taught Helena to love.

With all my heart, I offer gratitude to my parents for the biggest gift of all - life. I love you unconditionally. Thanks also to my sister Valerija and nephew Kevin, who help me relax me and remind me of the joys of my childhood.

I owe many thanks and praise to my colleagues, friends and fellow leaders: Kristijan Krautberger, Marjan Tinauer, Roman Toplak, and Brane Recek. They believed in me and my vision from the very beginning. You are the ones who make our enterprise one of the most successful in this field.

Thanks also to my friends and fellow leaders from Celje: Toni Jezernik, Alen Marič, Jože Kernež and Marjan Rudnik, who joined just a little later. You created columns that helped support our enterprise. I have learned a lot from each of you, Thanks also to Robert Viraj for introducing me to these great people.

Thanks to all the beloved spouses and girlfriends of my colleagues. Without your support, understanding and love, we would not be what we are today.

I owe thanks also to all our sales representatives for informing people daily of the route to a successful financial future and for spreading my ideas. You are the ones who make us grow and constantly improve.

Thanks to Andrej Okreša and all our office staff. You are a great help and support to me.

To Kristina Planjšek, Darja Koren and Ines Robič, who sometimes work day and night so that the sales representatives get their salaries. You are my sunshine. Thanks also to Mirjana Bolt who brought a lot of new energy to our company.

Thanks to all who believed in me and helped me at the very start of my business such as Mitja Mejač, Vladimir Vrbnjak and Gregor Bogme. Special thanks also to Andrej Osterc, Denis Stroglio, Marko Podlogar and the rest of the Merkur insurance company. You prove that the highest level of cooperation is always possible. It has been a pleasure to work with you.

Thanks also to Mr. Sebastian Žlebnik and the rest of the employees in the Generali insurance company, and to Mr. Marko Vončina and Uroš Skuhala and everyone else at the Maribor Insurance Company.

Thanks to Matej who worked behind the computer when we needed it the most and to David Gorišek for providing his valuable computer knowledge.

Thanks also to Milan Krajnc - Pavlica who helped us at the start of our journey.

Thanks to my schoolmate and friend, Kristijan Prostran; your drive was a major motivation for me. In many ways, you revealed secrets of the ways to a better life for me. Thanks to my friend Matej Čer. From you, I have learned what I needed the most.

I will never forget the years we lived together. Thanks also to Mirko Prusac who taught me the basics of positive thinking.

Special thanks also to all the participants of my seminars; I learned a lot from you. Thanks also to all the volunteers who helped me organize our motivational seminars through which we are blessed to change people's lives for the better.

Thanks to everyone who has been on the edge of despair and shared his or her problems with me. You allowed me to put my knowledge into practice and are the proof that my techniques and methods really work.

Thanks to Mrs. Jožica Tolar, manager of the Youth center in Maribor and her teachers who trusted us with their pupils. The seven days we spent together are a memorable highlight along our path.

Thanks to all the children from the Youth center in Maribor - you are my inspiration. Thanks to my coach Boris Vene; being with you expanded my horizons. You have been there when I needed you the most.

Thanks to Marko Goran Lorencin, my personal fitness coach who led me toward my maximum physical wellness.

Sincere thanks to Mojca Poljanšek, who worked day and night so that this book could be published on time.

Thanks to Alfi Hutter for your consistency and perfectionism in creating this book. Thanks also to my friends Nikola Grubiša and Franjo Trojnar; your books gave courage and confidence when I needed them the most.

Thanks also to Susan Jeffers, whose book *Feel the Fear and do it Anyway*, helped me through a time when I was very depressed.

Thanks to Anthony Robbins, the great world expert in the psychology of change and personal growth. You and your seminars, books and audio programs altered my belief in my capabilities.

Thanks also to the rest of the world-famous experts in the fields of personal growth, sales and marketing. Your ideas helped me to form the knowledge that I share with others. Finally, thanks to whoever supported me in any way in my work who has not been mentioned. You should know that I love you all.

Your friend and colleague, Smiljan Mori

CONTENTS

Foreword 15

Secret #1: The Way to Motivation 25
Personal and Spiritual Development 25
Developing Direction 26
Developing Self-Image 43
Developing Self-Confidence 56
Developing a Life-Long Love of Learning 66

Secret #2: The Motivation Magnet 81
Turning Dreams Into Reality or the Art of Setting Goals 81

Secret #3: The Roots of Motivation 131
Emotions 133
Satisfaction of Basic Human Needs 134
Fear: the Virus of Success 155
The Three Agents of Emotions 162
Techniques to Overcome Fears and Phobias 190

Secret #4: The Heart of Motivation 193
The Story of Your Life and Mine 195
The Department of Overeating 204

The Department of Mental Diet 210
The Department of Giving Up Smoking 213

Secret #5: The Source of Motivation 217
Relationships 219
Forgive - Forget - Get Healed 219
The Department of Effective Communication 225
Attitude Toward School and Study 234
The Department of Raising Self-Confident and
Independent Children 239
The Department of Love 244

Secret # 6: The Fuel of Motivation 251
New Approaches to Motivation 253

Secret # 7: The Treasurer of Motivation 287
Career and Money 289

The Conclusion 321

About the Author 325
About the Smiljan Mori Companies 329
About the Smiljan Mori Programmes 331
Recommended Reading 337

FOREWORD

In these pages hides a great treasure.

It was a December evening two years ago. I had an appointment for a meeting with Smiljan and the leading men of his company. Because I had overheard "stories of his success," and I knew him from before, I was looking forward to going to Štajerska. I was thrilled to be meeting people who were business savvy and so successful that they were known all over the country.

The meeting was about three hours long, the people were more professional and pleasant than I had anticipated. It was good. We talked about certain problems and simple solutions for entrepreneurship and a better life.

Within a few months, I was surprised by a phone call from Smiljan. He thanked me for that evening... because "it allowed him to increase sales in his company by almost 100%."

Incredible...a company already so successful increased sales!

One hundred percent!

Based on one meeting!

Then I realized that it was because of a special organization, furthermore, because of a special leader.

It was not I who helped him to increase sales.
He did that himself.

Honestly, I was simply "singing my song," as DeMello says, as I had been singing it to many other companies (and most of the time, there were no such successes.)

A good leader has to sense the right information, listen to it, accept it, transfer it to his people and motivate them so that they are able to change existing patterns and habits within their work. If you have ever had an experience trying to make such a change, then you will know that it is not that easy...

But not for Smiljan.

It does not surprise me that his people are so successful. They could not have a man for a leader who knows more about this philosophy than Smiljan Mori.

What I like about him the most is that he lives what he teaches others. There is not much talk, but a lot of action. He teaches by example, not with "information". He is living proof that anything is possible. He is sorry that he took out a loan for a car instead of investing in his education. He is most likely the first one to take the matter so seriously that he traveled all over the world to check out for himself how the best do it, then knew how to bring the best knowledge to the ungrateful (sorry, but we do deserve it sometimes...) Slovenian market, where foreign experts are more respected than Slovenian ones.

He was the first (at least to my knowledge), who managed to pack big halls with his seminars.

In addition, within a few months, from an "unknown local businessman," he was transformed into one of the best known, most appreciated and in-demand motivators.

That is Smiljan.

Today you hear about him at every step. Not only from the participants of seminars, but from "ordinary people" who have experienced his wisdom, energy and compassion. His name is spoken with respect, because he proved that Slovenia isn't small.... only those who think so are small.

FOREWORD

His big heart, clear message and capacious knowledge will bring a smile of joy to your face... and also maybe a tear to your eyes.

I believe that all of us should be thankful for this book, which could mark a milestone in our literature. And I'm sure that it will become a hit. And now it is up to you to feel, to receive the message and use it in your everyday work. If you do need help, go to the seminar, which will give you so much energy and drive that you won't know where to start first because you'll have so many ideas and solutions (that has been my own experience!).

Read the book. Many times. Follow the message and don't allow yourself to be caught in one of the most insidious traps of our mind - in the sentence: "I know that already."

I believe that you do know a lot already. But that is not the point... It's about whether you live this information, and if it becomes your everyday routine. Here lies the difference between a winner and an average person.... So, the purpose of reading this book is to get the energy and motivation to bring changes into your life and allow them to lead you to happiness.

As they did for Smiljan.

And there is something more – don't be misled into thinking you must imitate his way. Do not try to follow him; that isn't the way to proceed; it's all about following your way... the way shown by your heart. Smiljan's way is just an example of what's possible. No two people have the same route to happiness, so choose the one which will lead you to pleasure, not to pain (which may happen if you try to follow someone else's way).

There is nobody like Smiljan... or you or me.

Then make a decision; turn to yourself and step out on the path to winning.

(Keep the book on the bedside table "just in case"...)

That is the most anybody can do for you.
You better believe it!

With love,

Boris Vene

INTRODUCTION

It was a cold November in 1996, when I learned I was declined for the criminology position at the school for internal affairs. The stated reason was simply "employment policy." I remember vividly how angry, insulted, and devastated I was at not getting that job. Not only because I really wanted to take part in developing research, but because I longed to share my knowledge with others. I really wanted to teach. I was overwhelmed by negative feelings of every stripe: rejection, loss of confidence, loneliness, depression, and perhaps most of all fear. I was afraid of the future. What would I do with my two diplomas in internal affairs? Even though I was an exemplary student I had nowhere to turn. Should I wait and hope for the school administrators to change their minds or should I?... I didn't know what to do. My possibilities were limited. Then I sat down for a long serious talk with myself. I'll never forget that conversation as long as I live.

I decided from that moment on that my future would depend only on me, not on outside influences or external forces beyond my scope. Literally overnight I quit the job I had since it wasn't leading in the right direction. I moved to work for the High Court of Ljubljana cutting my income in half, back to entry level salary. It was hard. Despite my multiple degrees, my income barely covered rent and food. Just to survive I worked for a real estate agency on the side - renting and selling property, books, and insurance. Then one day I realized that somewhere along the line I had lost my drive for being an attorney or even some day... a judge. Instead, I decided to start my own company. Trouble was I knew I'd be doing this with little or no financial resources of my own, mostly because I had nothing.

My family freaked out! Rightly so, I was broke and supposedly trying to explain to others how to invest in themselves. I survived those times thanks to my mother who 'donated' gas money every month, so I could go on. Despite all the obstacles, I was convinced that there is a path or track to success worn in by those who travel ahead. I searched for attainment by learning from those worthy to follow. Not accidentally, Susan Jeffers book *Feel the Fear and Do It Anyway* fell into my hands at just the right place and time in my life. Her words gave me a renewed sense of power, energy, and confidence that I desperately needed to overcome such hard times. Because I believe so deeply that those who travel ahead carve a path or track toward success, I decided to take a closer look at the insights, choices, and ideas of those who make their lives meaningful, who make effective choices, and take conscious action. However, much has changed since then, when I was 25.

Since then I've grown two companies. My first company grew into a leader in the financial and insurance business in Slovenija. I worked side by side with Kristijan, Marjan, Roman, Branko to make this happen. Not long after we were joined by Toni, Alen, Marjan, Jože and others. I travel all over the world - Europe, the US, and Australia— with the sole purpose of discovering any traits or attitudes common to successful people.

But wait— hang on a second, 'successful people'… what is that? What does that mean, 'successful people?'—Well, for me, it meant earning well, living well, evolving happily, content, satisfied… yet not complacent. When I feel great appreciation, activation, and positive momentum toward my goals, then I experience success in my mind. When I'm unruffled, energized, and feeling alive, I feel success in my body. When I have no regrets, few misunderstandings, and no animosity, I feel success in my heart. That's how I think of 'success.' Then everything I discover I put into practice, try it out… I keep what works, throw away what doesn't, and keep growing with positive results. I've listened to most leaders in personal development —Anthony Robbins,

INTRODUCTION

Jerry Coffe, Art Berg, Jurgen Hoeller, and John Gray— and had the great pleasure of meeting a few.

Now I offer my own motivational seminars in Slovenia, Russia, and throughout Eastern Europe. I've been an honored guest on various television and radio shows providing insight and motivation to viewers and listeners. I've written articles discussing the techniques I've gathered for helping others help themselves to overcome fear and self-limiting beliefs. I've helped people break through their own emotional blocks. Psychologists and psychiatrists even began taking interest in my work. I've provided personal consultation for professionals in many fields, including businessmen and athletes. The national women's ski team invited me to be their personal motivation coach in 2002. Universities and secondary schools have invited me to guest lecture. I also offer corporate courses aimed at motivating employees, developing successful sales methods, and leadership in the 21st century. After almost nine years, my dreams have realized.

The result of my success is that, as my dreams become reality, my old beliefs about reality shatter. This means that somehow the best is yet to come. I've moved into a realm beyond my previous ideas about how the world operates and what was possible for me. Only now I realize they were limited, although they seemed far-out and wild… nine years ago. I've come to realize that what you become is far more valuable than anything you might possess. My goal is not to keep rambling on and on, trying to convince you that I'm some kind of miracle boy, something special, unique or different from you. I just want to share how once upon a time I was not simply broke, but I was living without vision, energy, dreams, or hopes. When I 'came to' and realized only I could be responsible for my own life, I asked myself some important questions. This eventually led me to study successful people and through that expressing my own version of success in life.

I wanted to find any secrets, strategies, or methods, common to successful people. Is success a creation of circumstances, or do successful people generate successful circumstances for themselves? Is there a hidden recipe for success, happiness, and contentment? These questions helped me to dig out the secrets I've gathered in this book.

Seven Secrets to MotivAction, is the cumulative result of books I've studied and the personal development and management seminars I've attended all over the world. This is the result of research and my own experience, as well as those I've learned working one on one with a variety of individuals. I've tested everything you'll read myself. According to my experiments… I can assure you everything works!

Doubts are healthy and normal. If we trusted everything, we'd be constant victims, always doing what we're told. That would be contrary to the essential goal of this book. It's all right to doubt what you read or hear. Healthy skepticism encourages you to test what you find, to weight the relevance and importance any idea has to your life. Years ago, I too doubted some of the ideas I describe. As I've studied, experimented, and seen the results in myself and others, my personal beliefs have… let's say, evolved. Nothing good would come of everyone thinking the same way all the time, or being in complete agreement on every issue. The only thing that's absolutely necessary is that you open your mind to possibility while reading. This is sometimes called suspension of *dis*-belief. This doesn't require full agreement, or alignment, or even understanding of all the ideas and methods set forth. It just asks that you suspend *dis*-belief. Even if you are naturally skeptical, approach the book with open neutrality. Only if you can be open and prepared to learn something new and perhaps

INTRODUCTION

unknown, can you master radical change in your life — for the better, of course! The goal is not to 'follow the rules' or 'memorize some affirmations.' I hope I will inspire you to forge your own trail, unique to who you are, where you're headed, and where you're starting.

The examples I use are from my own life. The experiences reflect real people, only a few names have been shielded by request. I invite you to share how you make changes that lead to progress in your life.

I discovered that success has a lot of so-called definitions, and for too many the idea of 'success' is not very well rounded. Some people who are successful are rich but not content. On the other hand, too many people are content but aren't without problems or limitations and complications rooted in financial issues. Through the years, I've asked myself... if everyone really even *wants* to be 'successful.' Wealth, financial abundance, may not be everyone's ultimate goal. Or they don't want to admit that their limiting perceptions about the *kind* of people they believe are rich... can create fears and blocks preventing them from facing their own misperceptions. While it is true not everyone wants or needs to become a millionaire, surely everyone wants to eliminate financial fears, worries or, especially, limitations.

Before reading further, I feel obligated to warn you that this isn't a book you can just read and put on the shelf. This book demands your participation. You'll find numerous interactive exercises that require full participation if you expect to see progress and transformation in your life. I suggest you read pen in hand, underlining, making check marks, or circling ideas you find particularly interesting and relevant to you. Mark the key concepts you find in various chapters and come back to them. Every time you reread chapters you'll find new aspects and elements that perhaps weren't relevant or noticeable the first, second, or even third time around. Keep a notebook or diary handy to jot down your own ideas, reactions, and inspirations as they cross your mind while reading. Reading it simultaneously with someone else to exchange ideas and experiences or exercises is even more effective. This adds meaning and dimension for you both.

Above all, I wish you reward and pleasure from reading this book. One thing is certain: it can help you achieve a happier, healthier, richer, more content, more passionate, more fulfilled life full of love.

With motivation to success!

Yours, Smiljan Mori

SECRET #1:

THE WAY TO MOTIVATION

PERSONAL AND SPIRITUAL DEVELOPMENT

"Whatever you can do, or dream you can, begin it. Boldness has genius, power, and magic in it. Begin it now."

J.W. Goethe

DEVELOPING DIRECTION

My excitement over my first plane ride shifted to panic when it suddenly hit me that I didn't feel safe... about fifteen minutes into the flight. I was hurtling through the air miles above anything familiar and worst of all, I had no control over the operation of the flight— at all. I knew we were headed to the Canary Islands, but I couldn't see anything except fog and ominous looking clouds. Not a vision offering much relief. It didn't make sense. When I drive I need to see where I'm going so I can steer. How can we be traveling without a clear view? I have on occasion driven into fog, barely seeing ten feet in front of me. This slowed me down, of course, but I continued moving forward, much more cautiously.

Getting there is a challenge, in and of itself... no matter what. Getting there becomes more difficult when there's no end in sight, nothing but fog and clouds and sky in every direction you look. Driving one foggy day, I ended up two hours late because I lost my way a few times. Although I was navigating and operating the car, I struggled to see where I was going. Obstacles only popped into sight at the last second, turn offs I needed were nearly invisible. I was on heightened awareness staying on top of things, reacting appropriately. On the plane, I found myself wondering how the pilot had any idea where we were going when he couldn't see a thing. I asked if I could visit the cockpit and look around.

To my surprise, the pilot invited me. He was kind enough to explain what some of the buttons and gauges did. He spoke in a relaxed, reassuring manner. He didn't even seem to be checking the flight's course. Dozens of questions crowed my mind: "How does he know we're flying in the right direction?" "What's our altitude?" "How does he know we're not heading toward another plane?" The pilot must have recognized my confusion because he explained:

> "The secret is AUTOPILOT. After I set our course and our altitude, we operate on AUTOPILOT."

'Wow!' I thought…'Is that all?'

Then it hit me: this is how we live, whether we're aware of it or not. At some point in our lives we engage the autopilot, letting it steer us through life. Sure, the ride may seem comfortable… until we bump into a problem. But, like our pilot, we can alter our course or shift the altitude of our life path.

Imagine for a moment you're on a plane headed for the Canary Islands. The altitude computer is set to "autopilot." This guarantees that the plane stays at the altitude programmed at takeoff. A feedback loop constantly adjusts the plane for wind speed and direction. If sudden gusts push the plane a little too high, the autopilot alerts the pilot to bring it back to the correct altitude. Like cruise control in a car, autopilot maintains the programmed details of the flight.

BELIEFS PROGRAM AUTOPILOT

Just as a plane's autopilot is programmed before takeoff, you 'absorbed' certain beliefs about yourself, about your strengths, your weaknesses, your capabilities, and your potential during your childhood. This initial information then determined your course. As growing and learning human beings, we develop the majority of our beliefs from information gleaned early on, some of which inhibits us from even attempting incredible heights or heading toward the goals we deserve or desire. Whether we like it or not, over time these beliefs compound to become deeply held convictions. These beliefs and convictions steer us… in fact, my convictions, your convictions, have steered us here, to where we are in our lives right now.

> "Some people have been sleeping for years; they switched on the autopilot and went out to have a cup of coffee."
>
> Smiljan Mori

It is impossible to alter or adjust the altitude or course of our flight without reprogramming our internal "autopilot." On occasion, circumstances or events may push us accidentally off-course… for better *or* for worse, but before too long, the self-adjusting "autopilot" will draw us back to our 'regular' course. For example, maybe you managed to lose weight for a while, but after a while you find you've lapsed into old habits and gained it back.

CHANGING COURSE AND ALTITUDE

The same rules that apply to the jet apply to our "autopilot." When we first begin taking conscious control of our lives, deciding we want change… too often that change is only superficial or temporary. Just as a pilot occasionally takes manual control of the plane, when we shift our attention and focus intently on a desired change, we take manual control… temporarily. Just as the plane eventually returns to its programmed course and altitude, we ultimately return to our old thought and belief habits.

REPROGRAMING YOUR AUTOPILOT

Creating changes in our lives demands we change our fundamental beliefs and opinions about ourselves. We will need to add new information. At this moment, we are cruising automatically at the altitude programmed perhaps by beliefs and attitudes swallowed up long ago. These beliefs set our course according to what our ingrained beliefs decided we deserve. We may not like the idea—but it is true. What we experience 'now' was programmed by our ideas about who we are and our beliefs about the world we inhabit. To create true and meaningful change, we have to take the reins of this truth and harness it in our desired direction. The fact is… if we keep making decisions based on the same-old information, things not only will not change; they simply cannot change. No matter how positive our attitude might be on the surface, no matter how badly *parts of us* desire change, nothing significant can happen. A positive attitude alone cannot create change. If that were enough, we could in theory think 'Table set yourself!' Of course, the table will not cooperate. To create meaningful effects, we must take action, and we must *do* something. To create true and meaningful change, we have to accept difficult realities and make challenging decisions from time to time.

HABIT AS A SUIT OF ARMOR

I often meet people at my seminars who say, "Smiljan; change is so hard. I have gotten used to doing things the same way over years of life. It feels like a suit of armor I just can't seem to get off." Sometimes I joke asking, "Have you tried a bit of WD40 on that?" This remark comparing habit to a suit of armor is incredibly insightful. People often describe their deeper unconscious thoughts and feelings in metaphors.

In this case, the metaphor reveals that this person feels trapped in a set of impenetrable habits. I also like this metaphor because it demonstrates the nature of why we develop habits in the first place. For the most part, habits of thought, reaction, and belief originally developed to help us in some way. In this metaphor, the habits were developed to 'protect.' Understanding this can develop a more effective strategy for reorganizing new habits that still meet these hidden needs. Taking the need for 'protection' into consideration when developing new beliefs will help this person build a system that keeps the old habits from coming back. In the 'feelings' chapter, we will discuss how our metaphors affect our feelings, our behavior, and our achievement in further depth.

> "Character cannot be developed in ease and quiet. Only through experience of trial and suffering can the soul be strengthened, ambition inspired, and success achieved."
>
> Helen Keller

THOUGHTS ARE MORE POWERFUL THAN THEY SEEM

To change a behavior permanently, we have to change the daily thoughts that feed the most complex and sensitive computer in the world, our brain. I am simply reminding us of something we already know; *our thoughts affect our body*.

This can be particularly evident during sports like basketball or golf. When a player misses a pitch or a basket they find themselves saying, "I just *knew* that wasn't going in." Not long ago, Miloš, from the Slovene basketball team, told me he simply could not make a basket from anywhere on the court anymore. He felt he was somehow lacking some sense of willpower. He described the feeling in his body when he missed the hoop as a stiffness in his legs. He was locking up, sensing failure in his body even before it happened. Whenever Miloš got in the position to shoot, his subconscious sensed failure. I taught Miloš how to replace his old mental pictures of failure with visions of success using thought repatterning techniques. We engaged sensations of self-confidence and certainty from other successful experiences, some from his past, and some from other activities. The positive results were clear during his next game, where he regained his sense of confidence and racked up the score.

> "The people who get on in this world are the people who get up and look for the circumstances they want, and if they can't find them, make them."
>
> George Bernard Shaw

SOLIDIFYING A HABIT

Let's investigate how habits are solidified and become permanent, whether they are helpful for us or not. Every action we embark on is the result of a thought created in our mind. What we think about determines our actions. Over time and through repetition, our actions become habits, and we know habits affect our overall behavior. If we keep repeating a certain thought or action over a long period (some experts say 30 days in a row), it becomes a habit. All habits have a profound impact on our behavior... and ultimately, our lives.

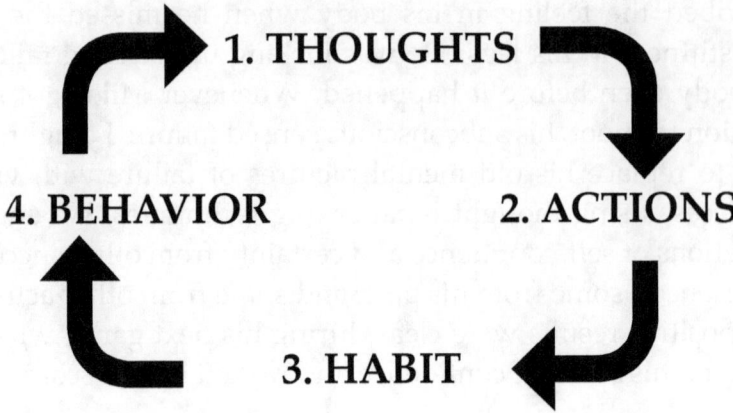

The good news is that no habit can become *so* deeply ingrained that it cannot be transformed. "It's a habit," is no longer a valid excuse for avoiding change. If we have been able to get used to something through time, energy, and repetition, we can also get rid of it the same way. We just start de-habituating ourselves!

> **"Habit is the best of servants or the worst of masters."**
> Nathaniel Emmons
>
> **"Habit is a good servant, but a bad master."**
> J. Jelinek

PERSONAL AND SPIRITUAL DEVELOPMENT

THE COMFORT TRAP

Over years of working with people of different backgrounds, professions, and belief systems, I've discovered that many people lack the passion to really do something remarkable or meaningful with their lives... simply because they've 'fallen asleep at the wheel.' It seems that once we find a manageable set of circumstances, once we create a routine, a pattern, we are rocked into a soft bed of familiarity, warm and comfortable. We settle into a familiar routine where there are few defeats, denials, rejections, or failures. Day to day, things tend to cruise along, not getting much worse, but not getting much better or, in fact, much different at all.

Others may achieve a lot in life yet somehow manage to let it all slip through their fingers because they 'fall asleep.' They fail to develop new strategies or adapt to changing circumstances; they fail to sustain the status quo or progress further in their careers or relationships. On the other hand, some people set and achieve amazing goals or a series of goals, but true contentment still eludes them. They mistakenly believe that achievement, or so-called 'success', would automatically bring contentment and happiness in their lives as well. When that does not automatically happen, they react by burying their head in the sand or hibernating. I have seen this happen to numerous salespeople I have worked with. They fall into the comfortable lap of success and are stuck. Despite their comfortable surroundings, they feel like a failure and are floating in a sea of discontent.

Sometimes, achieving our number-one goal creates a thin veneer of satisfaction. We settle into a comfortable routine with how much money we earn, the brand of the car we drive, our bank balance, the labels in our clothes, the vacations we take, and in our relationships. We convince ourselves we should be happy with placating self-talk like: "I'm pretty comfortable right where I am;" "I don't need more;" "I don't have time;" "I'm too old…too young…too [fill in the blank];" "Others live worse;" "I don't have the right degrees;" "I have achieved a lot."

These platitudes (a politer name for excuses) pollute or even poison our inner garden of success spreading weeds of delusion that eclipse our potential.

Often I meet incredible businessmen who have achieved major success in lightning speed. Despite this, they battle invasive, sometimes overwhelming feelings of discontent. Although there are thousands of people who would gladly trade places with them in a heartbeat, these achievers are unhappy. They fell into a comfort zone. No matter what their level of success, once they reached their initial objectives, they slip into a comfort-induced slumber.

The way to motivate, to shift beyond this comfort zone, is to set renewed standards and goals. I am not talking about goals that compare us to others. On the contrary, in that direction lies madness. To move beyond the comfort zone we need only ask ourselves if we have dug deep enough within ourselves and acted with all the potential we are capable of. We need to consider if we've honestly lived up to our goals, if reaching our goals brought us the rewards we anticipated. We can't be too afraid to consider that these old goals may be outdated, ill-fitting, or simply wrong for us. Did we sell ourselves short? Bite off more than we could chew? Go too far in the wrong direction? But the first challenge is complacency.

I experienced a version of this complacency, this comfort trap, during a recent training session with my coach Goran. We were working the leg muscles after I'd had a few weeks off. This break shifted me into a comfort zone. The usual exercises were harder than I remembered and Goran was having me repeat them ten times, each! On about the fifth one I started complaining, asking Goran, "Why are you tormenting me like this?" He only replied, "Because you can do it."

Gah! I hate when he's right. Sure I knew I could do it. After all, I had done it just two weeks ago. So I stayed with it and simply tried harder refocusing all my energy and attention on the task at hand, instead of wasting it arguing or complaining. "Wahoo!" Next thing I knew, I'd made it to eight —then nine— and ten! Had I been working out alone I might have been tempted to quit at the fifth repetition, when the going got rough. No one would have known but me. But if I had, I certainly wouldn't have experienced the satisfaction I gained from hard work and persistence. No matter how small this victory seems, every such act of persistence and determination, each act of integrity, builds a mental history, an emotional experience we can refer to anytime the 'going gets tough.' At that moment with Goran I determined that I'd apply the same maximum investment I showed toward in that workout to other areas of my life. That means I exert as much intensity as I think I'm capable of... plus 30%.

Psychologists call this *supramaximal* effort. This is a level of maximum effort with the added boost of "psychological synergy," or positive intent combined with refined focus. This turbo charged level of effort lies latent beyond the alleged levels otherwise described as 'maximal effort.' *Supramaximal* effort is the way to shatter conditioned responses and engage renewed determination. Too many of the restrictions people face day to day are rooted in fear of failure (or success), or in reenacting previous experiences of failure. Restrictions are the result of their own limited beliefs they have complacently accepted.

Another aspect of supramaximal effort is the illusion of 'broken' secondary assets. Let's say Marco feels he isn't capable of starting his own business because he's 'bad with numbers.' His math skills are a secondary asset Marco believes he lacks. In my case with the exercises, the secondary asset I lacked was drive. I managed to engage supramaximal effort, to turbo charge myself by fishing for another secondary asset to replace the one that was failing me. I called on my inherent stubbornness to replace my lacking drive. I exchanged one secondary asset for another to make the magic happen.

Marco might have other secondary assets lying around that he hasn't considered as replacements for his 'broken' number skills. Some possibilities are that Marco may be particularly good with directions and instructions. He could learn or re-learn the math he needs by referring to books. Or perhaps Marco has excellent people skills. Perhaps Marco could find a partner to help him get off the ground. Too often a broken secondary asset allows people to believe mistakenly they are limited in some way. Well, the good news is—secondary assets can be replaced!

There are three methods for engaging supramaximal effort. The first is through exercise, practice, as with my example of physical exercise. Every time I engaged my supramaximal effort, I assured myself I was strong enough, that I had the necessary resources to handle anything. The second method of engaging supramaximal effort is by imagining, pretending, or going through the successful motions. Since the mind cannot tell the difference between imagination and experience (at least at first) this imagining creates a library of positive memories of supramaximal effort. The third method is to remember, in as much rich and vivid detail as possible, a past experience of using your supramaximal effort. This extra vivid remembering of an experience from the past can create a new 'truth' that takes seed in the unconscious mind.

Imagine for an instant what you might create in your life if you gave your all, all the time! Don't be shy, take a look at every aspect of your day to day life. Imagine vividly the benefits of your efforts! Don't wait; right now, immediately, while the juice is flowing write down everything you might achieve if you always gave your personal best to life. Write it down now so you can be surprised by the results. When you make the commitment to transform any perceived limits, you start creating new thought patterns, a new pathway to your goals. You transcend beyond the old self that you could have, should have, and would have... if only...

EXERCISE 1: If only…..

What could I create if I offered my personal best every day?

_____
_____
_____
_____
_____
_____

EXERCISE 2: Secondary Assets

We can often discover the secondary assets we believe are broken, or just severely damaged enough to hold us back, by looking at our rationalizations, our 'excuses' for not... for not making that change, taking that chance, trying the extraordinary, taking that trip, painting that canvass. The reasons we tell ourselves for NOT doing, accomplishing, or creating [fill in the blank] in our lives. For this exercise, jot down a few 'reasons' off the top of your head. If you don't have any right now think of the most common reasons you hear.

For the examples, 'Kristina' is listing reasons why she won't go ahead and take that Swing Dance class she's been talking about...

Reasons, Rationalizations, (excuses)

I don't have a partner

I'm not a good enough dancer

I would embarrass myself

___

___

Now, identify the "Secondary Asset" each excuse claims is broken.

No people skills

No kinetic body skills

Low self-esteem

___

PERSONAL AND SPIRITUAL DEVELOPMENT

_____

_____

NOW think of other 'Secondary Assets' that might replace or 'bolster' the broken one:

I do have friends, who have friends

Replace with 'stubbornness'

Replace with 'passion'

_____

_____

THE PULL OF 'THE COMFORT ZONE'

To demonstrate how strong ingrained habits and patterns , try this:

Clasp your hands in front of you as if in prayer. Now take note of which thumb is on top (left or right). Then switch the thumbs, putting the first on top. How does it feel? More than likely it's uncomfortable. You may even have to struggle to keep from changing back. This demonstrates the potential discomfort of every new thing, or every change you may bring to your life. At first, it will feel strange, maybe even uncomfortable, but as with anything… you get used to it.

Do you remember your first try riding a bicycle or driving a car? In the beginning, you were thinking about ten things at once. Eventually, though, pedaling and steering or using the gas and brakes became second nature. Fear of moving beyond the comfort zone is natural. Everyone who has ever tried anything but was afraid to fail and hurt their pride, understands moving beyond the comfort zone. Imagine what the world might look if, when their toddlers had their first fall parents said, "Don't try anymore, give up, you'll just keep hurting yourself… besides, you'll never walk anyway." How long would it take you to give up on your child when he's learning how to walk? Would you wait a year, thirteen months, two years, three? Most likely, you'd answer. "I would never give up… I'd help my child try over and over again until he walks." Now you've discovered the magic formula for success, happiness, and contentment.

WHEN THE STUDENT IS READY, THE TEACHER ARRIVES

We interpret this to mean we attract the people, events, and problems we need to learn from. That means life itself is our best teacher. But it can be the toughest as well. One of my most important and perhaps most challenging life lessons is realizing that I attract all my "TEACHERS" and they usually come disguised as confrontations, annoyances, or disappointments. When I came to terms with this, I stopped feeling like a victim. To truly understand this lesson you must become attuned to the idea that the world around you is your mirror. You see the world through THE EYES OF YOUR OWN FEELINGS. Everyone does. It's a fact of our mechanisms of perception. When we find ourselves complaining about other people, what they're like, what they've done to us… we are truly only criticizing ourselves. We find mirrored in others the fears and limitations that loom large in our heart and mind. The good thing is we also find in others and in our experiences the positives and potential we hold in our heart and mind.

PERSONAL AND SPIRITUAL DEVELOPMENT

> "Everyone and everything around you is your teacher."
> — Ken Keyes

Keep in mind that every person you meet, that every situation you find yourself in, that everything that happens to you is a reflection of your own state of being, but also an experience, a situation, a scenario from which you're meant to learn. Keeping these two facts in mind will make change easier to manage.

MY TEACHER

My last "teacher" came just at the right moment, precisely when I needed him the most. Just an hour ago before I sat to draft this section, as a matter of fact. I called the barber. He said they had a vacancy, so I went. But then I ended up waiting 45 minutes. When I'm working, when I'm deeply involved in something, I can hardly stand to stop. But I had seminars to give and was getting shaggy. I had to get my hair cut. As I sat... waiting... even though I was told there was an opening... I started thinking through anger and anxiety. I let loose in my mind words expressing my negative emotions. But... since I teach others to steer their emotions, I managed to change direction fairly quick by asking myself a question...'what I was learning from this.' I know intellectually that what was happening was of my own making, my own design, just as all the positives are. As soon as I asked myself the question... I got an answer. Just yesterday I let one of my colleagues wait for *me* for nearly 30 minutes. The teacher *always* comes at the right time. The real question is if we're ready to face the sometimes not so flattering truth the lesson offers.

This idea resurfaced recently, as I was working with a client who asked me for input about his upcoming wedding, and the fact that he was married twice before. Along with his question, he commented that there were 'no women' that suited him. I congratulated him on his pending nuptials and wished him every happiness. He kept asking me for at least one bit of relevant advice. So I simply reminded him that throughout his life, he'd been attracting women into his life who reflected some aspect of his own personality, some aspect that brought something he needed to learn to the surface in the relationship. I reminded him *he* should be learning something from each experience. When he still persisted in pressing me about why he had no luck with spouses and why he seemed to always choose the wrong one, I explained that we attract people and events that mirror how we feel about ourselves. That only when his self-image improves he'll attract kinder and more loving women and situations into his life.

When I asked if he really wanted to get married a third time, he said: "Of course I do!" I simply reminded him that, "To avoid another divorce you must realize that this marriage is for life. During more difficult times in your marriage, you have to remember the saying, 'When the student is ready, the teacher arrives.'" He needed to be fully conscious, fully aware of the fact that he chose this woman as his wife in order to learn the lessons he needs most.

Do you find the same scenarios happening to you over and over in your life? Do you wonder why you keep stumbling into the same kind of people you dislike, making the same kinds of complaints about events, finding the same faults in every situation? As soon as someone starts criticizing another I ask, "What bothers you most about him?" This starts a long list of things they dislike about other people. My follow-up question is always, "Is there anything you could learn from them that

PERSONAL AND SPIRITUAL DEVELOPMENT

applies to your own life?" After a few seconds, almost everybody agrees that while others bother them, they could definitely take more responsibility for managing their own shortcomings. Let me finish this with the thought:

YOU LEARN MOST FROM THOSE YOU WANT TO CHANGE THE MOST

Stop wasting time and energy wishing to change others and start changing yourself.

> "When people find out how hard it is to change themselves, they'll stop trying to change others."
> Smiljan Mori

DEVELOPING SELF-IMAGE

DEFINING SELF-IMAGE

In essence, our self-image is a combination of ideas, beliefs, and opinions we've accumulated about ourselves over our lifetime. All our beliefs about who we are, what we can or can't do, about our experiences, and our reactions to our surroundings, all contribute to our total self-image. Beliefs that limit us and keep us from creating or experiencing *more* in life I call LIMITING BELIEFS. These are beliefs we haven't necessarily processed consciously. Yet we do have the power to free ourselves from them, consciously. I know from my experiences watching others that when someone changes their self-image, their whole life changes.

Do you view yourself as a self-confident, determined, and warm person that everyone enjoys chatting with? Or do you see yourself as shy, timid around other people? Do you see yourself as a positive person who seeks to discover only good in others? Or do you focus on other people's negative aspects? Do you see the glass half full or half empty?

Your self-image, your own opinion about yourself, defines the boundaries of your achievements in life. Whatever has happened, whatever you've experienced or endured in life, has happened. You can't change the past no matter how much you desire it or how hard you try. You have no influence over that past. The only thing you can influence is your reaction, your feelings, beliefs, and opinions about what happened to you. The importance you invest in events determines how you feel and what you ultimately choose to do. At one seminar when I asked, "Is there anybody who feels like they're completely struggling, just swimming against the current and barely making it right now?" Jasna stood up. In tears, she explained that she was abused throughout her childhood, and her life no longer made sense. She tried to commit suicide once already, but failed even that. Because Jasna found no meaning in her life, she would keep trying, keep repeating the same patterns of reaction, the only patterns of reaction she knew until she succeeded.

This shook me up since I care deeply about the well-being of those around me. I invited Jansa onto the stage to demonstrate several of the most powerful techniques for transforming pain and pleasure, and shifting the significance of past events. Eventually, she promised herself and everybody there that she'd never consider suicide again. Instead of continuing to believe that she was worthless because of the terrible things she'd experienced, Jansa became our teacher. She added a profoundly moving and

PERSONAL AND SPIRITUAL DEVELOPMENT

powerful experience to the event that affected everyone there deeply. No doubt, in comparison to Jasna some of the others seeming problems and challenges faded into the background in the face of this painfully naked honesty. Jasna created a positive momentum at the event as a result of her courage. Before she left that day, Jasna realized that she had the capacity to be an example, to help others overcome similar problems. Because of what happened to her, she rose to a stronger level of self-perception.

> **The importance you invest in certain events determines how you feel and what you ultimately choose to do.**
>
> Smiljan Mori

Not long ago I received a beautiful surprise from Jasna. The effects of her token kept me awake late into the night. Jasna brought me a portrait she painted of herself representing her awash in beautiful sunlight. This depicted a new aspect of hope and connection in her life. On the back of the painting, she wrote: "Smiljan, thank you for the hope! I love you, Jasna." I sat on the edge of my bed in tears. The happiness and gratitude I felt in my heart moved me deeply. I felt blessed to have been present when one young woman came to recognize herself as she truly was. With hope, her life will spread that hope to others. The feeling when you help someone to a happier and more contented life is the true gift! I'm sure that you, too, have changed someone's day for the better with a pleasant word or kind gesture. Savor those feelings and remember them often.

ROSE COLORED GLASSES

We determine the quality and accuracy of how we perceive the world and events around us by examining the nature of the glasses through which we observe. We decide whether we look through the eyes of optimism or pessimism. The world itself doesn't change on a dime according to our moods. What changes day to day, minute to minute, is us; how we see the events of our world is our choice.

> "We always find what we are looking for: good or bad, problems or their solutions."
> John M. Templeton

Our self-image determines the path our autopilot steers us in, and the speed and altitude we travel at. Your self-image determines the path and quality of our life. Take the wheel firmly in hand and re-direct it toward the open skies of opportunity, joy, love, trust, happiness and playfulness. Don't be like so many others who've remained sleeping for years.

CHANGE YOUR SELF-IMAGE; CHANGE YOUR LIFE

Just as the pilot can take back control to change the altitude, or set a new flight plan, we can redirect our lives by shifting our self-image. To control the altitude manually the pilot needs to keep vigilant watch over the autopilot. To change the autopilot for good, he'll need to re-program the system.

We have the same choices. To create a new altitude or set a new course for our flight, we must reprogram our autopilot. Our autopilot is our self-image. Like a pilot, we have two choices for changing the altitude of our flight: we can either take manual control and sustain vigilance or program new commands into the computer.

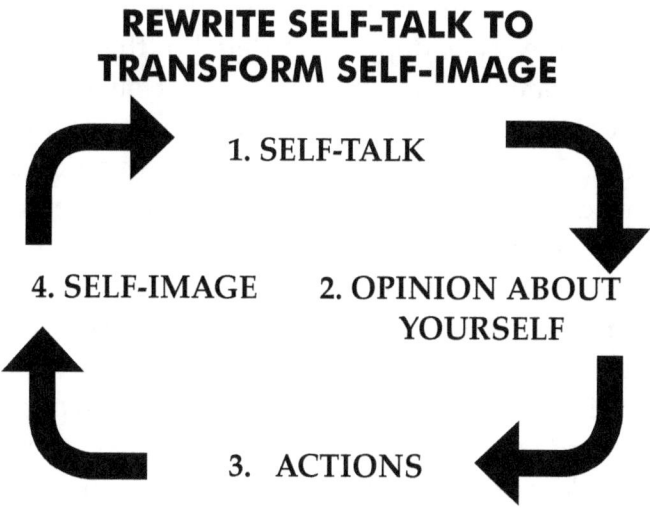

REWRITE SELF-TALK TO TRANSFORM SELF-IMAGE

1. SELF-TALK
2. OPINION ABOUT YOURSELF
3. ACTIONS
4. SELF-IMAGE

As it is shown in the diagram, self-talk, or the way we communicate within ourselves to a large extent determines our self-image. Occasional bouts of positive thinking don't have much impact — like rain in the desert. To improve and permanently shift to a more effective self-image, we need to manage our self-talk on a day by day, sometimes minute by minute basis. We build up a successful self-image *or* destroy what we're building at every daily interaction, by our choice. Yes, you read that correctly. You and only you are responsible for the quality of your self-talk and therefore, your self-image. No one else can get inside your head to manage your self-talk, or self-image for you. How we talk to ourselves from day to day impacts our autopilot programming... which in turn determines how high we can fly and the difficulty or ease of our course.

RECURRING MENTAL PICTURES

Most of us tend to think in pictures. When we listen to others tell a story, we usually create mental pictures, vivid images in our minds. We envision or 'see' people, colors, space, and distance. We detect cues for these images in another's tone of voice, pace of speech, and manner of talking. The words they choose contribute to the style, depth, and detail of the mental pictures our minds create. Words are triggers that elicit the replay of specific mental images. While you're listening to someone relate a story, tell a joke, or describe their vacation you create images in your head, *and* your subconscious records a mental video of these images you've created and store it along with the script. Over time, certain words develop correlations to mental images and emotional responses. When you hear the words again, they trigger a recurrence of certain mental pictures… and the corresponding emotions. Over time, these recurring cycles of stimulus words and emotional responses make deep tracks in our minds like ruts in the road that keep us stuck in the same repeated feelings or emotions, over and over and over.

Answer these questions to gauge the nature of your automatic image associations:

- Where did you take your last vacation?
- What's your bank account number?
- Do you remember the last funeral you attended?
- What's the best gift you've received for your birthday?
- Imagine someone who challenges you with donkey ears and a flower pot hat?

How fast did your mood shift as you read the questions? It probably took only seconds for your mood to change. Why? Because certain words triggered certain pictures to come to mind that, in turn, affected your emotions. The mental images stored in your mind control your feelings; therefore, the choices you make—, therefore, your destiny.

A few months ago, I met Lydia, a wife and mother of two. She'd been having trouble sleeping. In addition, her high level of anxiety had her losing so much weight that she ended up in intensive care. She was taking medication for depression, insomnia *and* anxiety. Because she'd tried to commit suicide twice in three months, she'd spent some time on a closed ward in a mental institution. When I met her, she was in a terrible state. Her husband was at his wit's end. He feared their only solution was institutionalization.

When I asked Lydia why all these things were happening to her, she explained that a few years ago something happened that reminded her of an early-childhood trauma. Since that reminder, Lydia cycled in and out of depression. Her weight dropped to barely 100 pounds. She ate literally nothing and had to be fed through an I.V. for a while.

When I asked her to describe the recent event that triggered the childhood trauma, she described it vividly with rich details. In her own mind, she'd pictured the unpleasant images that triggered negative emotions in full Technicolor. This demonstrates how we direct and produce the movie of our life, including our emotions and feelings. We record our mental images and replay them over and over and over ad nauseam… all our lives, even if we don't like them—even when they make us angry, upset or in Lydia's case, physically ill. I asked her if she'd keep going back to a movie theatre to see the same movie 1,000 times over, even if it shook her up, upset her, or made her sick. She said no… of course she wouldn't. My next question was, "so, why do you keep watching the same repellent movie over and over for the past 16 years even though it's hurting you?" Lydia was speechless.

The intensity of the pictures she was re-experiencing, trapped her in a corresponding set of destructive emotions. She hadn't laughed for months; her body was shrinking; all the muscles in her body were tensed, and she clenched her teeth so hard she was almost impossible to understand when she spoke. After almost three hours of engaging image-shifting and scrambling techniques of double dissociation, Lydia was set free from fears and phobias that had haunted her for years. That afternoon Lydia smiled for the first time in months. The trigger words that engaged her negative images and emotions were replaced by images and emotions that didn't drain away her life energy.

> "We are the directors and producers of our own life's movie, including our emotions and feelings."
>
> Smiljan Mori

Within a month, Lydia surprised everybody who knew her, including her psychologists and psychiatrists, by checking out of the hospital on her own and starting on a new road to happiness. Lydia stopped repeating the recording of her 16 years experiences every day. She no longer used specific words that triggered the replay of negative images and emotions. Sometime later, as she was vacationing with her children, she sent me a message: "Greetings. I'm having a fantastic time. I'm as overwhelmed with happiness as a young child!"

I'm no magic hypnotist or supernatural healer. This story simply shows how each of us get embroiled in problems through our own thoughts. We can overcome them the same way.

These patterns can stem from how we respond to our mistakes or failures. If when we make a mistake, or experience a setback, and we keep repeating the scenario over in our minds, blaming ourselves for it, dwelling on it, telling our friends and colleagues… we end up creating even more word-triggers linking to those negative mental images. This then adversely affects our emotions and negatively influences the actions we choose to take. Next thing we know, we try to lighten our load of guilt and shame by spreading the blame onto others. We may start accusing other people or blaming circumstances for our reactions, instead of taking responsibility for our feelings. Ultimately, we decide which movies will run in our own mental theatre. Choosing better ones allows you to feel better in an instant.

> "When a human is going through extreme events, it may occur to him that days are passing like minutes or minutes seem long like days, years, or eternity. It may happen that we aren't aware of where we are."
>
> Abraham Maslow

Dwell in the memory of the best moment in your life. Close your eyes and visualize that moment. Pay special attention to your visions of the people, the movement, the words, voices, and emotions. What do you feel? Do you feel motivated and excited? Happy and relaxed? While replaying positive events, start creating new trigger associations by telling yourself how wonderful you feel. Positive self-talk evokes other positive emotional states and helps you develop a better self-image.

SELF-IMAGE - YOUR BEST FRIEND

Think about how often we say things like:

- "You idiot, how could you do that?"
- "I'll never get ahead."
- "I'm ugly; no one will ever want me."
- "Only the rich get richer, and I am not rich."
- "I don't have what it takes."

What would happen if we talked like this to our friends? We probably wouldn't have many! So how can we allow ourselves to say things like this to our true best friends: our own self-image and self-confidence?

In general, 70% of our inner self-talk is negative. Why? Because when we were children, we didn't have the tools to filter out negative information. Before age seven, a child receives between 140 and 150 *thousand* bits of negative information. Yes, you read correctly. This negative information begins quite inoffensively with our parents saying things like: "no," "not that," "not now," "stop it," "you aren't," "never," "be careful," "you can't do that," and "watch out." In contrast, children before the age of seven receive only 3 to 4 thousand bits of *positive* information.

Although negative instructions may be necessary in early childhood for safety and survival, they still have an echoing impact in later life. That's one reason why we need to reprogram ourselves later, so we can feel more naturally optimistic about our goals, our actions, and even ourselves. Negative inner dialogue harms our relationships with others as well. On those days we find ourselves reacting negatively or feeling depressed, we should pay extra attention to the nature our inner dialogue.

PERSONAL AND SPIRITUAL DEVELOPMENT

POSITIVE SELF-TALK FOR SUCCESS

One message that repeats in almost all personal growth or self-help programs is that our self-talk determines our success in life.

Do you remember the moments in your life when you weren't very successful? When someone asked you, 'How you're doing?' You may have replied, "I'm hanging in there" or "not too well" or "I'm struggling but still sinking." Such responses not only let the other people know you're not doing well, but those feelings of hopelessness and depression double back on you making your bad mood even worse...

Here are two methods for harnessing and improving the quality of your self-talk:

THE 7 - DAY NOTEPAD

Over the coming days, for at *least* a week (if not longer) keep a small notebook and pen handy. Find something small enough to conveniently keep in a pocket so you actually use it. Every time you catch yourself experiencing negative things or indulging in negative self-talk, write *everything* down. Write down all the random words you hear in your mind.

In the beginning, you'll notice your list of negative thoughts and words seems to grow and grow the longer you keep track. It may seem defeatist to keep jotting them down, but don't give up. The only way for you to change them into positive self-talk for good, is become fully conscious of the array of negative thoughts, feelings, or reactions you engage in.

When I did this exercise for myself the first time, I was shocked at the number of negative thoughts and feelings rattling around in my mind. As I paid more careful attention to them, the number of negative words and thoughts seemed to increase. After a few days, I noticed something interesting. My negative bouts occurred mostly in reaction to reading something negative in the newspaper, hearing something negative on the radio, or seeing something negative on TV. By mapping my negative thoughts, I discovered a specific relationship to some action I was taking. Hmmm, interesting. I also noticed the same thing happened if I socialized with negative people.

So I decided to take action. I replaced all the negative stimuli with positive ones. For almost five years, I've been replacing newspapers with books and replacing the radio with learning audios. That doesn't mean that I don't read newspapers at all or listen to the radio. I used to read the newspaper front to back. Instead, now I read only the items that are of direct interest to me. I discovered that for me it's more than enough to read the title, subtitle, and short summary. I find out the details sooner or later or from other sources. I find I save a lot of time this way that I can use for studying material from my field, or other disciplines that catch my imagination. I've also developed a selective approach to which people I allow to influence my life, especially the circle of people with whom I associate.

TURN AROUND

EXERCISE 3: Turn Around

Make a list of the most common negative or negative self-talk statements you use. Since no one is going to read this, you can be totally honest with yourself. After writing them all down, it's time to turn them around. Take each statement and find a way to flip it, turn it around, or turn it inside out to create a positive statement. You are creating an "antidote" for each negative self-talk statement that will eventually neutralize the old negative statement.

Here are some examples:

NEGATIVE SELF-TALK	POSITIVE SELF-TALK
I'm completely exhausted.	I feel great.
I'm just a loser.	Each day is getting better and better.
Life is so hard.	I enjoy my life.

The first important step helps you isolate and identify the kind of negative self-talk that's weakening your self-confidence and therefore, weakening your ability to achieve. The second step neutralizes your negative self-talk with antidote statements that you engage whenever you catch negative self-talk arising. When used effectively these techniques create a powerful mechanism for reducing the harmful effects of negative self-talk. *Any* reduction in negative self-talk improves self-esteem and quality of life.

> "Language exerts hidden power, like a moon on the tides."
>
> Rita Mae Brown

DEVELOPING SELF-CONFIDENCE

SELF-CONFIDENCE - KEY TO SUCCESS

"Our inward soul is often compared with the outer reality of others."

Constantly comparing ourselves with others will never improve our own self-image or self-esteem. But without comparisons, how can we determine whether we are self-confident enough or not?

Sure it's easy to find out how much we weigh, just step on a scale. But we can only discover the true depths of our self-confidence by diving deeply within ourselves and honestly assessing the opinions and beliefs we have about ourselves. You can't hide from yourself, and no one else can step into your shoes to feel what you feel. There are numerous tests or quizzes that may help you find out your level of self-confidence, but in the end, the only thing that really matters is how you *really* feel about yourself deep down. Let's take a deeper look at how your self-confidence operates.

SELF-CONFIDENCE ACCOUNTING

Our self-confidence account works much like a regular bank account. At any moment, we can make a deposit or withdrawal. And just like a bank account, our "self-confidence account" can suddenly be in the red if we withdraw too much without making enough deposits. When I see someone exhibiting a low opinion of themselves, I think: "His self-confidence account is too deep in the red."

As with our financial bank account, we are the only one with access. No one else can make a deposit or withdrawal from our account. It is easy to imagine at first, that there are lots of other people who can make a withdrawal, but that there aren't many who can deposit into our self-confidence account. What about the people we encounter who is rude, or outright mean? What about people who criticize our work or offer disdainful assessments of our appearance by their reactions? In reality, these external stimuli can do nothing to our account, one way or another, until we choose to react or not. It is our reaction that determines whether an event or scenario will benefit or deplete our self-confidence account. In truth, you are the *only* person who can deposit or withdraw from your personal account of self-confidence. When you realize that, you'll take the wheel controlling your self-image and your destiny.

THE WORLD IS YOUR MIRROR

I'll never forget the advice given to me years ago. A friend said to me, "Smiljan, if you would like to know what people are like, ask them what bothers them the most in others. That's the quickest way to discover what they want to change about themselves."

Maybe we've experienced a day like this... arriving at work and everyone seems somehow depressed, unsettled, or angry. First, we must ask ourselves what is our own mood at the time. We usually see people and the world around us depicting or reflecting back what *we feel*. When we are excited and anxious, everybody around feels jangled and nervous. Whenever something about others bothers us, we must first assess our own state at the moment.

> "We don't see things as they are but in the way we are."
> - Talmud

Let me entrust you with four very important facts:

1. Before somebody else can love you, you must love yourself.

2. Before you can love others fully, you must love yourself. Not in an ego feeding, self-praise fashion, but simply by accepting yourself 'warts and all.'

3. The only thing that counts is what you think about yourself. Why care what other people think about you?

4. You can fool, lie to, and cheat others for a while, but you can never fool, lie to, or cheat yourself. You will always experience the consequences one way or another.

PERMISSION TO GET UPSET

More precisely, I'd like to explain that no one else can upset you as effectively as you can. Too often we give others (such as parents, a spouse, friends, colleagues, or even our children) the power to influence our feelings and thus impact our self-confidence. Of course, people will agitate us from time to time, and affect our self-confidence and self-image, but be aware that they can do that only after we **give them permission**. Yes, you read correctly; you **give them permission** to upset you.

Just as we give other's permission to disturb and upset our self-confidence, we also must *give permission* for the compliments and praise of others to influence us positively and make a deposit in our "self-confidence account." We tend not to accept critics, but we also tend to be suspicious when someone pays us a compliment or offers us praise. We immediately ask ourselves "What do they want from me?"

YOUR THRESHOLD

Have you ever woken up feeling irritable after a poor night's sleep? You just kept tossing and turning. When morning came, you felt as if someone hit you with a hammer. You struggled to wake up, forced yourself to get ready, and dragged yourself to work. You were running late (of course) and in a hurry. The car ahead of you suddenly hit the brakes turning left without signaling. You almost hit them! What do most of us do? We start shouting… "You!#$&=&/ stupid idiot!" Have you reacted that way too?

Here's another example. You have a beautiful night's sleep. You wake up rested and satisfied. There's plenty of time to eat breakfast, listening to some beautiful music, and then calmly make your way to work. Along the drive, you notice the budding trees; you think about nice things waiting for you at work… someone takes advantage of your relaxed state suddenly cutting ahead of you. How do you react? Most likely, this time your reaction will be different. Most likely… you'll just let it go telling yourself, "They must be in a hurry; no problem."

Do you know anyone who has a really bad temper? You might be tempted to say they have a low threshold of patience. But the truth is they have a low threshold of self-image. A persons' greatness is measured by what they encounter before becoming upset.

Three weeks before one of my seminars, I went to a learning seminar in Australia myself, leaving my colleagues at home organizing the details of the seminar. On my return, as they reported the results of their campaign, everyone was tense and quiet. When I asked what was wrong, they told me they'd been sending out company invitations for the seminar, but the database they'd been using had the wrong addresses." Now I understood why everyone was so upset. With heads down they eventually told me, "We wasted nearly 5 thousand dollars!" After that... silence. After a minute or two, I asked, "So what did we learn from this?" The question took them by surprise. At first, there were few responses. But after a few minutes, they started telling me the lessons they had learned. My next question was, "What will we do now?" They threw out one excellent suggestion after another, which they probably would never have thought of if the crisis hadn't occurred. Long ago, such news would have upset me, but now I just ask myself questions aimed at drawing different results. Instead of getting upset, I use opportunities to ask questions and learn from any experience, no matter how seemingly negative. Such an approach yields far better results than losing control.

It's not events or the comments or reactions of other people that upset us. The only thing capable of upsetting us is the significance or the importance we give to events. Yet another serendipitous coincidence: a few days ago, as I was struggling to put this short chapter together... this message arrived on my mobile phone:

LIFE HAS NO MEANING BEYOND WHAT WE GIVE IT

EXERCISE 4: The Meaning of Life

Think about it. What significance do you assign to your life events and situations? Which scenarios upset you, make you blue or depressed? Take a few minutes to write down all the things that upset you over the last week. Were they big or small things? Were they important or unimportant? Can you notice patterns or associations? What significance did you give them? Do it now:

The events that upset me last week:

Just a reminder— I encourage you to take advantage of all the exercises in the book. The ideas in this book can help you make significant progress. I wasted nearly two years reading books and promising myself I'd get around to do the exercises later… when I had the time… or when I finished the book. But I ended up never doing them. Eventually, I realized that reading without taking the action steps weakens the potential power of the information.

The time spent considering how the issues apply directly to you engages the complex mechanisms of the unconscious and the intellect to work together. In addition, the kinetic influence of writing adds to this powerful combination of processes. These reflective and kinetic activities build on the intellectual understanding you gain from reading, the personal insight from applying the concepts to yourself, and the new images recorded by considering another perspective. Besides, motivation without action has no meaning. Do yourself the favor of participating in the exercises before continuing. By writing your notes and thoughts in the book, you create a JOURNAL OF YOUR SUCCESS that allows you to recognize your progress over time.

PERSONAL AND SPIRITUAL DEVELOPMENT

YOUR PARTNER'S ROLE IN YOUR SELF-CONFIDENCE AND SELF-IMAGE

Married people or who are living with partners ask amazing questions about self-confidence and self-image at our seminars. The most common question is, "How can I cope with this negative person I'm married to (or living with)?"

I met Ivan, who *really* wanted his wife to participate in a seminar because they hadn't been in agreement for years. As far as Ivan was concerned... they were on the verge of divorce. He wanted to know, "How can I convince her to come on this journey with me? When I return from a seminar or event I've attended and want to share the ideas with her, she says, 'You've just let yourself get all hyped up again... it won't last long.'"

I'm not entirely sure how he did it, but eventually he managed to convince her to come. They attended the next seminar together, as a team. They reported that they found a way back to loving one another again. Breaking through the petty resentments and built-up misunderstanding, by thinking about life, themselves, day to day situations in a *new way*, they cleared the decks. For the first time in years, they understood each other as well as they did way back in the beginning of their relationship. As a bonus, Hilda's internal changes brought about external changes in the shape of 20 lost pounds. Transforming this challenge has positively influenced her self-image *and* her relationship with Ivan. The happier and more satisfied Hilda is, the clearer and more openly she can respond to Ivan. I've received an abundance of these kinds of letters. This shows that there are innumerable couples willing to improve their lives, themselves, and their professional lives... together.

While Ivan might grow personally and make his own kind of progress, if his wife weren't doing the same, the transformation may only be superficial or may drive them further apart. A spouse or partner has that strong of an impact on your reality, the quality of your life, your world and therefore, your self-image and your self-confidence. If a partner is not growing personally as well, how will they be able to encourage you in your growth, or understand your new actions and behaviors? Everything will seem unfamiliar to them. We know what the strange and unfamiliar do to people... it engages their habitual reaction patterns, it 'pushes their buttons,' excites their fear and anxiety. They may even obstruct you, find fault with you or throw blame at you, in defending themselves from the foreign, the unfamiliar they see happening in you. They simply won't understand the true reasons behind your choices.

Let's say, for example, you have a brand new tiny seedling that just poked through the dirt. If you bring it in the warm house, you have to make sure it gets enough light. If you leave it in the ground, you have to make sure it gets enough warmth and water. For the seedling to thrive, you have to provide the right environment. Your growing sense of self-image and self-confidence will require a proper environment in the early stages. As you progress, you will become stronger and more resilient. There's no denying that your partner or spouse plays a huge role in this environment.

DO YOU APPRECIATE HOW MUCH ARE YOU WORTH?

Many people tend to underestimate themselves and tell themselves that they are worthless, that their lives are meaningless, and so on. There is no end to the negative self-talk. we can be capable of. Think about the following questions:

PERSONAL AND SPIRITUAL DEVELOPMENT

1. Would you give both of your eyes for 1 million dollars?

2. What about half a million dollars for each hand?

3. Would you like to earn an additional 1 million dollars for the left and right legs?

4. Would you turn over your brain for 10 million dollars?

These amounts are regularly paid for accident's claims or damage lawsuits to victims. However high these amounts seem you'd hardly be willing to substitute cash for your biggest treasure - your life and a healthy body. I'm sure that you wouldn't give yourself up even for *millions* dollars. Which means your body (and yourself) are worth more to you than you think. You appreciate yourself more than you may believe at first glance.

You are something unique and wonderful. There is no one with specific knowledge and experience you have, therefore, no one else with the precise power you have. The question is what have you done with it so far? You were just born into this specific series of events to gain this power, through your own free will and choices to this point you've guaranteed that your experience is completely one of a kind. Be grateful for everything that you've seen, heard, and experienced. Be grateful for all the potential you are born with. Here are some facts that will amaze you:

The body changes 2 zillion cells of tissue every day.

In less than a year, you change 98% of the atoms in your body.

- Your skin recreates itself every 20 days.
- Your stomach is replaced once a month.

- You reorganize and replaced your bones once every three months.
- Your liver turns over every six months.

In other words, you're constantly changing. If you didn't like yourself yesterday, there's hope for you. You decided to progress in your life.

DEVELOPING A LIFE-LONG LOVE OF LEARNING

Congratulations on your persistence! If you have been reading the book and performing all the exercises, my sincere congratulations. That is a clear indication that you would really like to make more of your life, and that you aren't one of those who talk a lot and don't do much. I have the feeling that we are similar in many ways, because we both have the same goal of improving our lives and the lives of others. You have reached a point where the decision on what you are going to do in the long term will be taken. That is the area on which I have spent a lot of time and money in the last five years. I invested a lot of time and money in my education and personal growth. Before you continue reading, please answer the following questions to find out where you are in your life at this moment.

PERSONAL AND SPIRITUAL DEVELOPMENT

EXERCISE 5: Evaluating your current conditions

QUESTIONNAIRE FOR EVALUATING YOUR CURRENT CONDITIONS

Circle the number that best, most accurately, and/or most frequently describes your behavior for each statement. Be honest with yourself, and remember that there's no right or wrong answer.

1-never   2-almost never   3-rarely   4-almost always   5-always

1. I take time to learn something new every day. 1 2 3 4 5 ____

2. I regularly read three or more magazines connected with my profession. 1 2 3 4 5 ____

3. I find learning new things unpleasant, difficult, or unnecessary. 1 2 3 4 5 ____

4. I read five hours per week. (Any category or combination of categories is ok here) 1 2 3 4 5 ____

5. While driving I listen to something enriching such as informational podcasts, educational audios or audio books. 1 2 3 4 5 ____

6. I read one additional magazine (not work related) regularly. 1 2 3 4 5 ____

7. I associate with people who's opinions are similar to mine. 1 2 3 4 5 ____

8. I see two programs related to personal or professional development per year.   1 2 3 4 5 _____

9. I attend two educational seminars or workshops each year.   1 2 3 4 5 _____

10. I'm involved in at least two educational projects a year (learning or teaching).   1 2 3 4 5 _____

11. I invest 2% of my income toward personal and professional development.   1 2 3 4 5 _____

12. I don't ask questions at educational seminars.   1 2 3 4 5 _____

13. How well I learn depends on how things are presented.   1 2 3 4 5 _____

14. I organize my time to leave room for something inventive once a week.   1 2 3 4 5 _____

15. I review my personal growth after attending a workshop, reading a book, or learning something new.   1 2 3 4 5 _____

16. I share my observations and ideas about things I learn with others.   1 2 3 4 5 _____

17. I sit in the back at meetings or gatherings.   1 2 3 4 5 _____

18. I'm busy with activities that expand my horizons.   1 2 3 4 5 _____

First total:_____ Minus second total_____ =

PERSONAL AND SPIRITUAL DEVELOPMENT

Then add your points by using the number you circled for each answer. Add them together and record your total on the 'first total' line. Add your scores for statements 3, 7, 12 and 17 together, and write in 'second total' above. Calculate your answer by subtracting.

Explanation of the results:

81-90 Excellent: You are a professional lifetime scholar. Whoever achieves this will surely succeed in life.

71-80 Very good: You have strong abilities for self-management of lifelong education.

61-70 Above average: You fulfill present experiences and will be inspired with the desire for success.

51-60 Average: This chapter will provide you with potential skills that can put you ahead of the others.

< 50 Keep reading to learn to develop stronger habits for lifelong learning.

Source: The 6 Success Strategies for Winning at Life, Love & Business - Wolf J. Rinke, Ph.D.

PERSONAL DEVELOPMENT IS CRUCIAL

No matter what your level of education, you have a limitless potential for success. There are ways to deal with limiting beliefs, like "I'm not educated enough to succeed." I do not want to diminish the importance of formal education, because it is the foundation for further spring boarding to personal and professional development. But there is no way to emphasize enough the importance of acquiring knowledge beyond that we learn at school. Perhaps even more so, there is nothing on the planet that can replace or squelch an inherent sense of natural curiosity. The depth and breadth of our knowledge itself doubles nearly every three years. What that extra content is made of, is up to us.

> "A man should never stop learning, not even in his last hour."
> — Maimonides

Think about the fact that most people have read only a little more than a quarter of a page a day over the last five years. Given that, it is not so surprising that many people walk around dissatisfied.

INVEST IN KNOWLEDGE FOR SUCCESS AND HAPPINESS

PERSONAL AND SPIRITUAL DEVELOPMENT

You may like to think you do not have time to read books. However, consider how much of your time you spend watching TV or listening to the radio or reading newspaper. Every day? Each week? All month? How much time do you fritter away in unproductive small talk? More than one hour a day? Then perhaps you may be among those who could make a monthly wisdom investment of up to 40 hours. How many books you could have read in that time? Probably, about two, if not more. Could your life be different if you read 12 books in a single year? Sure, if they were the right books.

Do you think you would have an advantage in your field this way? Maybe you would earn more money, more efficiently, then you would be happier; you could spend your time doing more of what you want. Do you think an investment in knowledge will pay off? When I talk about reading books, I mean those that offer guidance for improvement in one or more areas of the "wheel of life;" meaning the variety of activities and people that combined make up what you describe as a full and satisfying life.

Do you spend eight hours a day at work? Earn just barely enough to support yourself and your family, if you have one? If you want to embrace and embody full rounded success, you have to invest in yourself. What is an hour or two more over the course of a week? The benefits grow as you become more efficient and insightful as a result.

> "Age wrinkles the body. Quitting wrinkles the soul."
> General Douglas Mac Arthur

1. INVEST IN BOOKS

I promised myself to be a life-long scholar, that I would read everything that might change my life for the better. However, I have not only been reading. I have tested the new approaches on myself. When I discovered a method that can help engender change for the better quickly, I passed them immediately on to others. In a matter of only a few months, thousands of people at my seminars will have experienced an astonishing array of advantages in their lives relative to a single idea. Even today, I read at least an hour each day. On vacation, I read as many books as I want; that is the joy of vacation. I invested in speed reading techniques to be more efficient. In the last five years, I've read more than 400 books, and each one of them has enriched my life. Books are the greatest legacy you can offer your children.

The first in a series of books that completely changed my point of view was *Feel the Fear and do it Anyway* by Susan Jeffers. It fell into my hands at the right place in time. I was hovering near rock bottom, limping around on crutches for almost a year from a football injury. I can see the benefit of that seeming 'accident' now…the injury forced me to become aware of myself on a very different level. I started to be aware of my life, taking stock of the consequences of my choices and learning to make new choices in a limitless field of potential. I started asking myself, who am I? Where am I going? Moreover, what is my mission?

> "Your car can be transformed into an audio-lecture hall on wheels."
> - Smiljan Mori

PERSONAL AND SPIRITUAL DEVELOPMENT

2. INFORMATIONAL AUDIOS

I always use the time I spend in the car listening to informational audios. If you spend as little as fifteen minutes twice a day driving or commuting, another ten or twenty running errands, then invest in a portable audio player of some kind. That is almost an hour a day. You could have been educating yourself 30 hours a month. Listening to audios now offers an almost unlimited variety of options. You can learn about everything from Renaissance Philosophy to current marketing trends either of which can add to your world view in helpful ways. I especially like to listen on my way to big meetings, in the morning as I get ready for work, and even while in the gym. This adds a dimensional bonus to my time spent working out. Sometimes I stay in the gym longer just to hear what comes next... it is guaranteed to be useful, educational, and more than likely fun.

3. VIDEO

There are available ways to access excellent video formats of lectures, speeches, seminars, and other forms of documentary information. From mail order DVD service to on-line viewing on YouTube... there are innumerable videos on expansive topics, from world history to future science, all of which may offer just the insight you need to ignite your passion or solve your puzzle.

> "If we are of the belief that we know everything already, we surely will not learn anything new."
> - John M. Templeton

4. SEMINARS

To integrate the knowledge you have accumulated into your everyday practice, I recommend attending seminars, events, gatherings, conventions, continuing education in the fields you are involved in and interested. If you are a motorcycle parts manufacturer who likes to meditate, you might go to the manufacturer's annual convention and take a meditation retreat. Both will nourish your inner quest for knowledge. Few things can compare to the three-dimensional 'Live- In Person' benefits of such events. You can absorb almost as much at a big live event as you could pull together by yourself over ten years. The additional interpersonal connections of a live gathering have exponential potential benefits. You experience all the new information physically, mentally, and emotionally simultaneously. There is a big boost to hearing the voice, speech pattern, and catching the vibrational sound and vision waves at a live event. How do I know? Because I attend between six and nine live seminar, events or conventions a year, beyond the ones I offer. In the beginning, I even borrowed from the bank to invest in this from of 'education.' I did not take out a loan for a car, but for the seminars, trainings, and events. I invested in the single best way to learn what I needed to know to pursue my biggest ambition. I now feel there is even more of value I am able to pass on to others as a result.

5. A DIARY

THE most important investment you can make is a personal diary for writing down your aspiration, hopes, and visions, as well as any ideas that come to you while reading, walking in the woods, drinking tea, or chatting with Grandma. Your diary becomes an invaluable resource of productive ideas if you use it effectively.

I record all ideas that come to me over the course of my day. When I read back the diary later, I am continually amazed at many ideas can be sparked from reading one page or having

PERSONAL AND SPIRITUAL DEVELOPMENT

one insightful conversation! Try it. If life is worth living, it is also worth being noted.

EXERCISE 6: Lifelong Learning Plan

Make a plan and contract yourself to fulfilling it immediately:

1. From now on I will read at least _____ minutes daily.

I intend to start by reading:

_____
_____
_____
_____
_____
_____
_____

2. I am going to find an audio-program to listen to driving to work, commuting, or doing chores.

I would plan to listen to the following audio-programs:

_____
_____
_____
_____
_____
_____
_____
_____

3. The seminar(s), lecture, convention, or course I want to attend in the next three months:

Seminars:

_____

_____

_____

_____

_____

Now do the research and find the upcoming date and cost…and register!

Date of Event:_____

Date registered: _____

_____

_____

_____

Now do the research and find the upcoming date and cost…and register!

Date of Event:_____

Date registered: _____

_____

_____

_____

_____

PERSONAL AND SPIRITUAL DEVELOPMENT

Now do the research and find the upcoming date and cost...and register!

Date of Event:_____

Date registered: _____

_____
_____
_____

INCREASE YOUR EFFICIENCY

Many people misbelieve that they must institute vast sweeping change across all areas of their lives to meet a major goal. I am explaining that you can, by building incrementally, transform your life by 10, 000% or more in as little as four years.

Let us take it to the numbers. Every day, five days a week, you improve some aspect of your approach or outlook on life by 0.5%. Within a month, you have transformed 10% of your experience. Within a year, the effects of compounding small changes day by day grows to 300%. Continue this way and you'll experience a 1,000% change in two years, more than 3,000% in three years, and an incredible exponential transformation by 10,000% has come about in only four years.

This is not a simple mathematic equation, but a complex interrelated geometric expansion. Each improvement joins with, crosses over, intersects, combines with... other changes, affecting even more aspects by reflection and proximity, until all aspects, all dimensions of your experience are improving. Many people have applied this approach to track improving efficiency in areas of their lives.

How much do you have to invest in the form of time, effort, or money to engage a 0.5% a day change in yourself? That is the equivalent of about ten minutes daily at a high level of focus. Do not forget: one single piece of advice, one idea, one sentence you overhear or read, one thought that catches your fancy somewhere, or one piece of constructive criticism can have a significant impact on your point of view.

It is possible to grow a hundred fold toward your dreams, toward your goals, and aspirations in only four years. When are you going to start? Where are you going to start? Tomorrow? Today is best, otherwise you will miss today's' potential 0.5. Start now! Why put off change? If you have been reading this for at least ten minutes today, give yourself a pat on the back… congratulations, you are on your way.

THE POWER OF KNOWLEDGE IS ACTION

PERSONAL AND SPIRITUAL DEVELOPMENT

Have you ever read or heard something interesting and thought 'hey that's incredible; I should...' but you didn't? Like what you just read, for example— could that change your life if you applied it? It changed mine and millions before me, and millions yet to come.

> "Information without action is a car without gas."
> - Smiljan Mori

Acquiring information is so simple. You can turn anywhere…the Internet, DVDs, audio and video programs, newspapers, books, magazines, blogs, and chats. The only problem is that **we gather and collect information but** fail to put any of it to use; we delay applying any at all.

SHORT STEPS FOR SUCCESS:

- This week go to the bookstore. Spend some time browsing through the variety of books available. You will be surprised at the amount and selection of information available, and the breadth of knowledge you can acquire from any single category.
- Research an available audio program. Develop a new habit of listening to the audio you have chosen in the car, running errands, or while doing chores at home. You do not need to be the victim of random music or mindless chatter on the radio; protect yourself from advertisement and engage in a topic you find interesting. Do not 'waste' time on local DJ banter or confrontational 'talk' shows. Feed your mind food of your own choosing not just random junk floating aimlessly in space waiting for an open receptor.

- In the next three weeks identify a skill you've been wishing to learn or hoping to master. Find out about seminars, courses, events, or conventions available at different educational locations and levels. Note them in your calendar and start putting aside money.
- Calculate 2% of your annual salary. This is the amount you should earmark toward personal development. This can include books, audio and videos, seminars, workshops, personal consultations, professional examinations, and any and everything else that can help increase your value and potential. The following year's investment should increase to 3%, the next year 4% and **the following one 5%.**

> "Two words change everything - START NOW"
> - Mary C. Crowley

- If you are a businessman or a manager, note that the American Society for Training and Development, ASTD recommends companies invest 2.4% of their annual income toward employee education.

Those are the kinds of investments that put you in the same category of the most successful individuals and companies in the world. Putting a plan like this it's a proven, well-worn path toward growth, expansion, and improvement that can't help but draw you upward, making probable your wishes will be granted, and your goals will unfold.

> "The main goal of education should be opening the windows through which we look upon the world"
> - Arnold Glasgow

SECRET #2

THE MOTIVATION MAGNET

TURNING DREAMS INTO REALITY OR THE ART OF SETTING GOALS

"We need long-term goals, which protect us from short-term failures."

George H. Bender

TURNING DREAMS INTO GOALS

One of the most beautiful and rewarding aspects of the work I do is that I contribute to the betterment of others' lives. Mastering this chapter means you need never feel lost, aimless and/or unhappy in your own life. To avoid falling into another comfort zone we reset our goals as we close in on the fulfillment of our old ones. I noted that the 'comfort zone' is a potential trap that can ensnare us anytime we reach the next rung on the ladder.

But to keep motivation and to sustain momentum, to keep the rally going, we need to look up…find our next hand hold and reach out for it. To keep going, we must first know precisely where we are going. Otherwise, all our energy, all our dedication, our attention spent is nothing more than wheels spinning in mud. Without a clear destination, we could be busting our butt doing nothing but turning circles on the same path, over and repeatedly.

To know always the next step, the next rung, the next turn off on our trail, we must, must, must know where we are headed. To do that, we need to examine our dreams, hopes, and longings to create goals.

EXERCISE 7: Evaluating the clarity and precision of life-long goals

For each statement, circle the answer you believe best captures your situation or describes your attitude or experience.

1. I know what my goals are; I do not need to write them down.
a) Yes
b) No

THE ART OF SETTING GOALS

2. I take time out to dream about my future.
a) Never
b) Until now, only once
c) Every five years
d) At least once a year

3. Government and educational institutions are largely responsible for our development.
a) Yes
b) No

4. Circle the statement that best describes you:
a) I do not have a clue what my life-long goals are.
b) I have never been taught/learned to develop clearly defined life-long goals or write them down.
c) My plans and goals are only necessary for the workplace.
d) I have seen many important people in my life, such as parents, or family, friends, or mentors use clearly defined personal goals that they write out.

5. My life-long goals are:
a) Nonexistent.
b) In my head.
c) Are written down somewhere special.
d) Are written and planned.

6. If you were to wake me up in the middle of the night and ask me what my life-long goals are, I would be:
a) Annoyed.
b) Shocked you are asking me such a question.
c) Clueless as to what you are talking about.
d) Eager to tell you.

7. The fear of failure is worse than the fear of success:
a) Correct
b) Incorrect

8. My life-long goals are (circle all that apply to you):
a) Written down in a place where I see them every day.
b) In my head, so that nobody can see them.
c) Written goals supported by specific, measurable steps.
d) Written goals supported by an action plan with key dates marked in my calendar.

9. My daily schedule depends on:
a) Tasks and needs that appear daily.
b) What my superiors tell me to do.
c) My own scheduled tasks.
d) My own scheduled tasks prioritized by and connected in some way with my life-long goals.

10. When developing a risky new idea, is the worst time to consider others' opinions.
a) Correct
b) Incorrect

THE ART OF SETTING GOALS

To determine your score add the number of points you get for each answer.

1a~ 0; 1b~5

2a~ 5; 2b~ 2; 2c~ 5; 2d~ 10

3a~5; 3b~ 0;

4a~ 2; 4b~ 0; 4c~ 5; 4d~ 10

5a~ 2; 5b~ 3; 5c~ 5; 5d~10

6a~5; 6b~ 0; 6c~ 0; 6d~ 10

7a~ 0; 7b~ 5

8a~ 5; 8b~ 5; 8c~ 5; 8d~ 10

9a~3; 9b~ 2; 9c ~ 5; 9d~ 10

10a~ 5; 10b~ 0

Total_____

Explanation of the results:

91 EXCELLENT: You are a master of goal setting. Please call me; I'd like to work with you.

81-90 VERY GOOD: You really know how to behave in a given situation.

71-80 GOOD: You have a solid base. Now is the time to start building on it.

61-70 AVERAGE: You will need to gain some more tools to help you focus on your lifetime goals.

<60 Lucky you! You will get much more from this book than you paid for it.

Sources: The 6 Success Strategies for Winning at Life, Love & Business - Wolf J. Rinke, Ph. D.

SCRIPTING YOUR FUTURE

The most important thing is that the future we create should help us not only survive but thrive in all weather…all the seasons of the year; spring, summer, fall and winter. Our goals should offer real leadership, provide us with meaningful guidance at key navigational points. Our goals should help us develop real success and contentment in life. To accomplish this our goals must be real. The only 'but' is… not all goals will bring real success *and* contentment.

> "For me, success without contentment isn't success."
> Smiljan Mori

Many so-called successful people are indeed constantly pushing for the attainment of higher and higher goals. They set their sight on earning a lot of money, becoming famous, being seen as adorable, having the best cars, houses, yachts, or villas. While I could never blatantly say… such choices are 'wrong,' because all that is good is there for us to enjoy. Sure… why not you? What I am getting at here is the 'Type A personality' constantly creating pressure, stress, frustration, and anxiety to keep the adrenaline flowing. This is a case of, "As in the higher the stakes, the bigger the rush."

Focusing solely on material gains tends to be wasteful because one of life's little ironies is that we inevitably enjoy the material fruits of our labor as we travel the true way to success *and* contentment. To focus only on the material gains is like planning a road trip across the country that will stop in all the most interesting and notable places but failing to get out of the car. Focusing on the exterior, the movement, the speed, the velocity means you miss all the highlights along the way. Having a meaningful final goal in your head *and* on a piece of paper means having something far more than mere material belongings or approval from others.

> "If you don't know what you would like to achieve in your life, you probably won't achieve much."
> John M. Templeton

THE KEY TO 'SUCCESS'

Is the goal of success to be rich, *or* healthy *or* happy? This is one of the great philosophical questions people throughout the centuries have endlessly discussed and debated. Sometimes feel we might be tempted to do virtually anything for success. That's perhaps a consequence of not even knowing what 'success' really means for us. Success, in essence, involves satisfying certain fundamental human needs, which differ from person to person. Some go so far as to so desperately connect with success, with money that they have agreed to do *anything* to earn it. They eventually end up unhappy. For others, money has less influence because they opt to direct their energy into family, friends, and relationships.

The trick is each of us must define our own 'version' of success for ourselves. The important thing is that we **know** what we want. My study of success and successful people has led me to this conclusion: to gain success, to be happy, content and rich, in more than just money but in a spiritual sense as well, one should gain mastery in the following areas:

- Health (including what we eat and moving and using our body)
- Emotions (including mastering negative and positive emotions)
- Relationships (including family, friends, colleagues, our social environment)
- Money (how to earn it, save it, and ensure it)
- Career (work that makes you happy), and
- Personal Spiritual Growth

We all tend to develop everyday routines that then become our trap. We get up in the morning nervous knowing the coming stress of the day; rush around to drop the children off at the nursery or school; rush to work, where we end up staying late. Work of course offers constant streams of stress, so we come home exhausted our minds still chewing the multiple problems posed on the job thoughts still at work. Because more than likely we were torn from our current task, unable to finish. This life revolves around only one…maybe two areas. All other aspects of life are shoved aside to deal with the most urgent and most important.

SUCCESS REQUIRES THE FOLLOWING SKILLS

1. Sales
2. Management
3. Time management
4. Communication

Most of us tend to spend an inordinate percentage of our time and energy controlling only one or at most two areas in life. Some of us manage brilliant careers that earn us lots of money but neglect our own well-being. We know very well that if our health collapses, all the money we have earned will go for medical treatment. All the money on earth is useless when we are not able to spend it. On the other hand, some of us have dedicated energy and focus getting and staying healthy; we participate in sports, eat healthy, even experience personal growth, but are constantly in the red in the area of finances. Some of us have happy family lives, but are dissatisfied when going to work under pressure. Some like to do "big things," but they do not have enough family support. TRUE SUCCESS requires that we simultaneously develop all these areas of life to live happy, contented, and successful.

EXERCISE 8: Wheel of Life

Mark where you believe you stand now in each area on the wheel of life. To determine your direction and generate progress you must clearly determine where you are standing. Therefore, it is important you be 100% honest with yourself. This is no time for softening the blow, denying reality, or protecting the ego. That is taken up enough time already…you can't achieve lasting benefits without starting in truth.

WHEEL OF LIFE

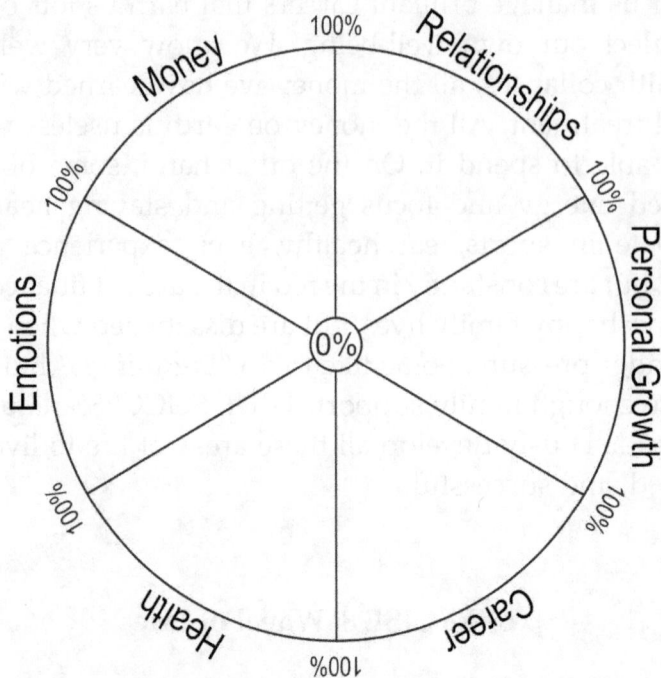

Remember strength lies in balance. Try working at a table with one short leg. Only by brining equivalent progress in all areas of life can you grow stronger and more flexible. Once all the wheels are the same size, and all pointed toward the same goal you gain a new sense of drive that can create things that you didn't dare dream about in your life.

LIFE WITHOUT A GOAL IS A RUDDERLESS SHIP

Too many people float aimlessly through life without determining a direction. Those who have at least 'some idea' rarely develop specific goals that will lead them toward their vague desire. Most people are not concerned with creating a clear purpose in life; they are just grateful to make through each day. It's taxing and difficult living day to day, month to month, paycheck to paycheck; like a leaf falling from a tree, going where the wind carries us.

Having nowhere in mind as a destination will get you nowhere... fast. Without a clear vision of your destination, the only place you *can* go is "nowhere." People never plan to fail — they just fail to plan, and that is why they fall prey to those extremely tempting 'comfort zones along the way. The 'comfort zone' starts to look more and more appealing and 'ideal' compared to a vast expanse of unknown territory. Without a destination, the plane is stuck in a huge fog bank. Without a destination programmed into the autopilot, the plane wanders aimlessly around the clouds running dangerously low on fuel, being worn out and tired, with no safe harbor.

> "If you don't have a clear vision of where you would like to go, you will reach "nowhere" in a second."
>
> Smiljan Mori

So what do I mean by all this talk of destination and measurable steps and goals? Planning a nice vacation is the closest example to what I am suggesting for your life plan. To go to a popular destination such as London, Venice, Greece, or Australia requires a lot of time research, thought, and planning. First, you need the paperwork, the credentials you will need even to take off: passports and or visas. You will need to determine activities for this vacation. Like it or not you have to pinpoint precisely where you will land, where you will sleep, how you will get around. You will probably have to pinpoint your transport connections to specific hours of specific days. You would never tell the chopper pilot to pick you up from your secluded island…sometime in 2013! The timing and coordination as well as the cost of your vacation travel probably required most of your planning time. These are the key factors you have to define first to plan the rest of your vacation.

Most people spend more time planning a single vacation for a few weeks out of their lives than they devote to plan their entire lives. Even the most astute executives often fail to define clear and specific goals on the job, have the wrong kind of goals; they are just not specific enough, or the goals are dangerously unrealistic. To make the most of our lives we need to engage at least the same amount of research, decision-making, planning, and budgeting we would devote to a luxury vacation to developing our life goals and life plans.

THE ART OF SETTING GOALS

> "To accomplish great things, we must dream as well as act."
>
> Anatole France

In Alice in Wonderland, the Cheshire cat asks Alice, 'Where are you going?' and Alice replies, 'I don't know.' The cat then points out that, 'In that case, any road will take you there!'

Like Alice, many of us do not know exactly where we are going. We may know a lot about where we ***don't' want*** to go, or to be...but not so precisely, what we ***do want***. We may get up in the morning only because we have to get to work. We somehow grapple our way through the day, get home to do our chores and eat, then and park ourselves in front of the TV to hopefully can 'get some rest' for our brains or maybe find some fodder for water cooler chat tomorrow. Then we fall into their beds only to get ready to do it all over again the next day.

This is how a how a ship without rudder sails? This is how the field for an archery competition in looks without targets, or soccer field without goal posts—blank.

QUESTIONS FOR DISCOVERING YOUR DEEPEST WISHES AND GOALS

EXERCISE 9: Who Am I?

In a few sentences, capture the essence of who you think you are. Include what you think are your best capabilities and greater skills? Describe your good qualities. Where could your sets of skills be successful?

These questions will reflect your opinion about yourself. Your opinion of yourself determines the potential success that you will experience. Do this exercise now. After completing the entire book, come back to these pages and answer the questions again. Your opinions, your ultimate goals, your aspirations and your beliefs about what you are capable of will be different by then.

1. I _____ am....

_____

_____

_____

_____

_____

_____

_____

_____

(After finishing the book or in a year's time)

I am..._____

_____

_____

_____

_____

_____

_____

_____

_____

2. What I Dreamed About As a Child

Can you remember childhood moments before you 'understood' what was and was not 'possible'… before the older kids or your parents or teachers, or life itself showed you otherwise? Did you want to be a doctor, a lawyer, a famous musician, or a top athlete? Perhaps you wrote to Santa Claus about specific things he should bring you, shiny guns to be sheriff, a nurse's uniform and stethoscope. Alternatively, maybe like many children, your parents "let you know" Santa Claus was struggling this year so there was little point in bothering him with your list. Perhaps it was that moment when you realized for the first time, that you would not always get everything you want in life.

Do you remember dreaming about beautiful houses, cars, nice dresses and unknown places you would someday visit? Exotic careers you would embark on? For just 5 minutes let your imagination spread its wings and remember or reinvent all the things you imagined having, being, and doing back when you thought there were NO LIMITATIONS, and there was no excuse in the world that could stop you from experiencing your dreams.

Jot down major images or things that stick out in your reminiscences.

_____
_____
_____
_____
_____
_____
_____
_____
_____

Do not be bogged down about whether what you are imagining is accurate or not. Simply ask yourself what you would do or learn, and where you would go if you knew that you could not possibly fail. Let us say an angel came to you and said, "Hey you've done such a great job so far.... We'd like to reward you with all-expense paid (in all possible ways)

_____

But you have to fill in the blank. Would you go to an Ivy League school all expenses paid? Would you take your children on a magnificent trip around the world? Would you spend six months learning to play the guitar?

I would...

_____
_____
_____
_____
_____
_____
_____
_____
_____

Five years ago, I let myself dream this way and then wrote down everything I wanted to have in my life, what I wanted to try, to learn, to create and to earn. In less than five years, I am living the life I planned for; I have even exceeded some of these goals.

As a child, I often dreamed about being a researcher and sharing what I discovered to help other people. I had no idea what kind of job or career fit those activities. So with my hopes in mind, I enrolled in the police academy. Only to find after much hard work and grit that working as a police officer was not the destination I dreamed about. So I studied some more this time at the Faculty of Law later working as a criminologist. Only then did I bother to say to myself, "This is going to be the real thing." I researched reports about crime and criminals to investigate fraud. In a way, I fulfilled my childhood vision. However, I was not satisfied. I then switched mid-career to work at the Ljubljana High Court of Law because I believed I could fulfill my mission. After a while, I learned even that was not the right place for me. So I said to myself, 'I will be a teacher at the high school. I'll work with students who want to go into the police and security business.' I thought there I would really be able to discover new knowledge and to help the students.

The thought of teaching truly inspired me. I rediscovered that what I genuinely wanted to do was research, pass knowledge on to others, and then watch them succeed. But that career never even caught tread… before I could waste any more time and effort in almost 'right' or kind of' meeting' the desires of my heart, my heart changed, and I decided to blaze a new trail for myself.

A few months ago, I gave a lecture about my philosophy of life at the High School of Business and Economics in Celje. I talked about the motivation to study and work, and about goals that everybody can achieve. I talked a bit about what my goals were over the different phases of my life. I remembered for them my main goal in childhood, which was to do research and share my discoveries. I asked these students, "Did I fulfill my goal of doing research and sharing by giving lectures?" They all replied in the negative. With tears in my eyes and a trembling voice, I said, "But I am living my dreams, researching success; studying human behavior and character. I motivate people toward better achievement. If I'm not mistaken, right now I am in a school giving a lecture, and that was indeed my big dream." "It's true," the students eventually agreed. "You did realize your mission; only the way it happened is different from what you set out to do."

That was nine years after painfully learning I was rejected to teach. However, this news did not ruin my dreams, it just changed them; my mission has lived on all these years in my heart, and every day I am closer to fulfilling my childhood goal. Even now, writing these lines inspires a few tears of joy because I am writing a book I hope will help people everywhere, and that was exactly my goal five years ago, when I let myself dream…

EXERCISE 10:

Current DREAMS, WISHES, and CHERISHED GOALS

Now come back into the present tense with all the reminiscence from childhood hopes to the knowledge you have acquired on your way to today. Putting it all together, take a few minutes to reassess what truly are your dreams, wishes, and most cherished goals.

_____
_____
_____
_____
_____
_____
_____
_____
_____

EXERCISE 11: What do I enjoy doing MOST?

WHAT IS MY FAVORITE THING TO DO?

At which tasks do you feel most cheerful and uplifted? Which activities let you forget the time? Include any activities you do that have this effect, whether you do it for 'money' as part of your job or career, or if you do them for your family, or just for fun. Given a few hours recreation time with no other obligations standing in your way, what would you do to relax, have fun, or to help others? This awareness can help you enter the job market aware of your best qualities and look for a position where you can put them to work to earn more money.

I, for example, I really have fun communicating. I like interacting with other people, motivating them, studying with them, sharing ideas, comparing research, writing, lecturing and, of course, I enjoy the time I spend with my family.

What is my favorite task or activity? The ones I enjoy most?

_____
_____
_____
_____
_____
_____
_____
_____
_____
_____
_____
_____
_____
_____

EXERCISE 12: If I had ten million dollars...

WHAT IF YOU HAD TEN MILLION DOLLARS?

What would you be spending your time doing if you were financially independent and never had to work to earn money to stay alive, to sustain your family ever, ever again? What if you had enough money, property, or investments that you could live without working? What you would do? Write down everything that comes to mind. What would you do if you were financially independent? Describe the feel of your life... in a place *beyond work*:

_____
_____
_____
_____
_____
_____
_____
_____

EXERCISE 13: If you had only six months left.....

WHAT IF YOU HAD ONLY SIX MONTHS TO LIVE?

In your head, create a sense of urgency. What would you do if you knew that you had only six months left to live? Would you start a business? Whom would you call? What would you leave behind as your legacy? What if you had only three months left to live? What would you do then? Write down everything that comes to your mind:

THE ART OF SETTING GOALS

_____
_____
_____
_____
_____
_____
_____
_____
_____
_____

Of course, the real question is... do you have any rationale for not doing these things today?

EXERCISE 14: The final evaluation...

Not to be morbid but I want you to dare to write down what you wish for and yearn for and have not yet discovered how to release. One of the most effective ways to grease the wheels for this profound exercise is to write your own eulogy... what would you like to hear them all say about you, your choices, and how you spent your life? What kind of legacy, what kind of mark do you hope to leave behind?

At your funeral, they will certainly discuss the big things you have achieved... so what are they? Who would express grateful for all you did? Maybe your wish is to be a well-known expert in your field. If so, let it out by what they all say about you after you are gone. have probably known many people who carried with them to the grave many unfulfilled wishes and goals. Do not leave this world with an unsung song in your heart.

I want to hear at my funeral:

> "Imagination is very important in human life. It can show us beauty, success and a desirable outcome, or ugliness, despair and failure. How it is going to serve us depends on our decision."
>
> Philip Conely

EXERCISE 14: Dare to Dream

WHAT WOULD I DARE TO DREAM IF I WERE GUARANTEED IT WOULD COME TRUE?

Concentrate on the one thing you would most like to have, to work at, or to achieve more than anything else does. Dream, dream...

7 STEPS FOR INTEGRATING DREAMS INTO GOALS

Many people never bother to set goals. They may not even be aware of that fact. But their subconscious keeps delaying the task with one excuse after another of how they'll do it later after... they've studied their so-called options... after they accomplish one small goal... it's always something. Is this one of the many potential reasons you have not laid out your goals or established your dream life? It is highly probable you had this sense of holding back, this fear of saying loud and proud what we *really, truly*, want *in our deepest heart of hearts* based on our previous experiences. For some people setting goals creates real pain. The pain is rooted in their accumulated experiences of failure. Add up all the many occasions we've wished for something, perhaps set a specific goal, maybe even gave it our all but then weren't able to achieve it for various reasons. Different people fail for different reasons. However, to a greater or lesser degree, all failure is associated with self-sabotage. The events, situations, or scenarios we unconsciously sabotage are those with the deepest associations to the largest, loudest associations of emotional, psychological, or physical pain.

Once upon a time, we failed to reach a certain goal and were infected by, "THE NEGA-VIBE." The nega-vibe attacks our subconscious infecting our self-confidence, our desire for success, our belief in ourselves, and our motivation. In fact, the nega-vibe can reach deep enough to infect our whole belief system. In fact, if we were raised in a heavily nega-vibe polluted environment in which adults or those we respected expressed repeated assurances of doom, failure, and impossibility...'No one in our family has ever gone to college, and neither will you!'—the nega-vibe outlook may be all we know or understand. All the positive, self-promoting stuff you have been reading thus far would sound almost like gibberish if you were raised in a deeply affected environment. Nega-vibes are dangerous long lasting toxins that lie dormant only springing into action to squelch any semblance of hope or possibility that tries to get past the guards with so-called 'practicality' and 'logic' before the positive hope even has a full chance to take shape in your mind. If a nega-vibe at one time ever reached into your autopilot program, it surely scrambled your hard drive. The only way to defeat the nega-vibe is to rid yourself of it completely. A single molecule of nega-vibe left in the system has such a powerful resonance of doubt that it's necessary to purify your ingrained beliefs and ideas about 'the way life is.' You know you need intervention; you need cleansing to purge yourself of the nega-vibe if you often experience procrastination, feelings of incompetence, have extended bouts of the blame game, or experience symptoms like disappointment, bitterness, or the dreaded 'chip on your shoulder', or you find yourself taken down by debilitating failure.

> "Be careful lest the virus of past failure infects the remaining healthy cells of hope which can grow into a story of success."
> - Smiljan Mori

We need to find ways to cleanse our thoughts of these painful old unrealized goals. It is imperative that we free ourselves from their grip. Our future depends on it! These burdens of past failures are like an invading plague that blocks any seeds of hope from growing within us to become our success story. Doubt and hope are mutually exclusive, like light and dark. Hope, like light, pierces even the deepest reaches of doubt but is so fragile, so tentative. To clear space for hope, to fertilize the ground for optimism, to grow momentum, and reap fulfillment doubt must be eradicated. Doubt, fear, and patterns of negative thinking, memories of failure must be eradicated.

Getting free from all levels of doubt and negative patterns is the ultimate goal. To that end, we are going to re-visit some places in memory. Do not worry for the first time perhaps remembering this event will be worthwhile. Far as I pointed out with some of the stories in this book such as those of Jasna and Lydia that replaying the past is a dead end; in some cases, a trap. The only reason to revisit is to revise. We are going to make friends with this old experience. We are going to embrace and accept this unhappy experience. We are going to *learn* from this experience and then let it go for good.

Remember the questions I suggested we ask when confronting any 'teaching' experience in the present. Do you remember? 'What am I learning from this.'

The fastest way to take the 'sting' out of any experience is to question it. (That is a universal bonus fact right there. Keep that handy.) The situation immediately changes shape when it becomes the object of observation. This is a physics phenomenon. Science has proven that matter has the potential to be perceived as either a wave or a particle depending on the attitudes and ideas of the observer. I.e. by 'looking' at something, in this case an event from our past, we immediately and irrevocably 'change 'it. The observer effect. Not only do we 'change' it, but we can influence the shape of the 'observer effect' we leave with our 'intent.'

I know; I know this seems like a lot, but we will go over it a few more times in different ways. So far, think back to the first chapter. In chapter one, we put in play some activating questions we can pose. In the first chapter, we asked the questions to inspire more objectivity in our evaluations of people and events, so we can better learn from them. By detaching or muting the emotional impact of an event, person, or situation…we can at least be more aware of our subjective slant. We used the metaphor of the mirror to describe the events and situations in our lives as teachers. If we look for what grabs our attention in the given situation and think about it, objectively detached from emotions… it will more than likely provide valuable healing insight into our own weakness and shortcoming we can heal and improve.

To engage the cleansing or purification process we ask questions of our past event(s.) We go back to memories of events, special events, formative events that shaped our beliefs and change them. We change them by the very act of observing them. We change them even further by turning the idea around. As we 'observe' the memory, we are also hitting it with an 'antidote' ray, an inverse, mirror image thought into direct opposition. These 'changes,' 'alters,' and 'transforms' the memory event into useful soil for planting seeds of hope. Revisiting the memories that shaped our convictions and beliefs changes the memories. The better the thought we carry in our mind while 'visiting', the better the 'change' our observer effect has. Removing the pain of a memory is permanent healing.

Changing a memory allows you to move forward from a completely new and redefined place, a place of new beliefs, new ideas, and renewed potential.

So, after all that long explanation, we are going to try it. Remember the goal is not to go back re-feel the anger, shame, upset, or fear and get stuck there again— this is not the point of the exercise. So before you start fooling around here in the unconscious, you should have mastered the art of neutralizing the 'hot' emotions in the present first (chapter one)… anyway, it's recommended that you master the exercises in chapter one before moving to apply the questions to memories.

EXERCISE 16: Neutralizing nega-vibes at the source

1. Write down unfulfilled goals from your past.

_____
_____
_____
_____
_____
_____
_____
_____
_____
_____

2. Write down how you went about trying to achieve at least one of these goals. What were your plans? Did anybody else participate in the realization of that goal?

_____
_____
_____
_____
_____
_____
_____
_____
_____
_____
_____

3. What actually happened? Why did you fail? Where did you go wrong? What were you thinking at the time? What decisions did you make?

_____
_____
_____
_____
_____
_____

4. Now get rid of the pain of the unfulfilled goals, transforming the memory by asking the question: 'What have I learned from this?' Apply the mirror metaphor and look at how the event, person, or situation revealed some blind spot, some weakness or error you had not noticed. Turn it around and let it go. You have now transformed and reabsorbed this resolute nega-vibe. It has been neutralized and removed from your system for good. It can no longer influence negatively your forward momentum.

_____
_____
_____
_____
_____
_____
_____
_____
_____

THE ART OF SETTING GOALS

5. Do I still need to pursue or fulfill this goal? On the other hand, has changing the memory event neutralized the issue?

___

Example A

1. Write down unfulfilled goals from your past.

   I ran for student council president in High School and lost.

2. Write down how you went about trying to achieve at least one of these goals. What were your plans? Did anybody else participate in the realization of that goal?

   I just heard about sign up to nominate yourself over the announcements, and I registered. Several of my friends were running for other things, and I wanted to go to after school meetings and help and see what it was all about. I got the required signatures. I made posters and made a speech at the assembly. I was only a sophomore, and the position was for all year. It usually went to a senior or a junior, but no one had been nominated for it. I really did not know that when I signed up.

3. What actually happened? Why did you fail? Where did you go wrong? What were you thinking at the time? What decisions did you make?

   I lost to a junior who ran away with it even against the senior. I was devastated. I was humiliated in my own head. I acted as though, aw shucks, on the outside, but I cried and felt absolutely destroyed. I think I decided I'd never run for something I wouldn't win for sure… but I've broken that as many times as I've kept it… I don't know.

4. Now get rid of the pain of the unfulfilled goals by transforming the memory by asking the question: 'What have I learned from this?' Apply the mirror metaphor and look at how the event, person, or situation revealed some blind spot, some weakness or error you hadn't noticed then? Turn it around and let it go. You have now transformed and reabsorbed this resolute nega-vibe. It has been neutralized and removed from your system for good. It can no longer negatively influence your forward momentum.

   I have learned to get the facts before committing and to rally support among friends first. I have learned that there is a season, a right time for pursuing some things… If the event was a mirror reflecting something back of me – it was probably I was carrying around a 'I'm going to lose' as soon as I realized the full nature of the race. I could have pulled out, but I thought that would look or feel worse. As soon as I was confronted with 'the truth' according to some… I immediately lost heart. The opposite would be—do not lose heart. Know the truth in full before getting involved, but make it your truth. Do not let the beliefs of others taint or infect your own.

5. Do I still need to pursue or fulfill this goal? Or has changing the memory event neutralized the issue?

    No need to pursue… even if it was possible. Finished!

There! I have effectively neutralized a once debilitating memory that was still influencing my decision-making process. Knowing that the event memory is now forever changed, you should ask yourself if you still need to achieve these goals or not. If the answer is no, then you can celebrate, because that failure was a great lesson and blessing for you.

> "We create our reality for ourselves."
> - Jane Roberts

Janko always wanted to be a lawyer. After graduating from secondary school with top grades, he wanted to study in Ljubljana at the Faculty of Law. However, it was too expensive, so he went to work for a reputable company. He could not have anticipated how adversely this would affect his motivation. Janko was successful at work but never gave his best. He was never able to feel any real enthusiasm for the job or the work.

When Janko did this exercise for the first time, he tapped this memory of realizing he would not be able to study law. It was back then that he established his attitude toward hoping, toward failing to get what in this case, he felt he 'deserved;' to study at a good school after earning top marks. He caught the nega-vibe of, "What is the point of getting all involved and excited- it doesn't get you what you want or what you deserve?" Every time Janko was tempted to get all excited, dig in and roll up his sleeves to work hard toward, this memory stopped him. It stung him and stopped him in his tracks. Feeling it just reminded him that long ago he yearned for something he did not get.

When he looked at this as a mirror of himself, he learned that perhaps he did not truly believe that he deserved it. Or maybe once others told him 'it was impossible,' he just gave up... did not even go part-time, but just gave up. What he learned was that if he really had wanted it as badly as he claimed, he might have pursued it more. What he learned was that possibly he was scared of going, maybe some part of him already feared that the competition at the big school would be too much, that he 'wasn't good enough.'

The observer effect neutralized this memory event, and Janko could let go not only of his own emotions and resentments about the disappointment, but also of the ill feeling he'd carried toward his parents, who he felt discouraged him at the time. Removing that brings him one step closer to a better relationship with his parents now; which has to be at least the equivalent of 0.05%. Janko got a whole day's worth of momentum on just this exercise alone... plus the neutralizing of the memory... which probably is worth at least as much, and so on, and so on, and so on...

ANOTHER WAY TO NEUTRALIZE NEGA-VIBES

This little process in exercise 17 is a great method of neutralizing nega-vibes; it gets them out from their hiding place and changes them for good. But what if you don't really seem to have a relevant memory event to work with for a particular issue? There are always more ways to do this work than I can possibly record, but these few will get you started. There are ways to achieve the same ends of eliminating fear, doubt, or painful negative experiences of ideas from destroying your hope and optimism for your future goals and plans.

EXERCISE 17

Write down all the goals you achieved when you were not even paying attention.

_____
_____
_____

5. If your achieved goals have gotten lost down the drain, recall them and celebrate now, because it is never too late.

6. It is of importance for you to get a feeling of triumph.

> "What minds conceive they can also achieve."
> -Anonymous

7. Do it NOW!

ARE YOU EVER TIRED AFTER WORK?

Do you ever come home from work exhausted? If so, you probably just want to sit down in front of the TV and relax. After briefly "surfing" TV channels, you catch yourself sliding into dreamland. you ever come home from work exhausted? If so, you probably just want to sit down in front of the TV and relax. After briefly "surfing" TV channels, you catch yourself sliding into dreamland.

There must be evenings when you get home even more tired, but a friend has invited you to a birthday party days before. You come home, get yourself ready, wash, dress in nice clothes and fly to the party whistling. Or perhaps you could hardly wait for the week to end because there was a lot of work to do at your job. Yet on Friday afternoon, you are suddenly in a good mood because you remember that at 6 PM you are on the road to the coast. You are full of energy and afterwards you dance all night long or stroll down the beach. Do you see the difference? Why? It is because you have new goals in front of you.

You can see how much energy you have just because you set a small goal. That is not even counting the excitement you feel at the time. All of this happens because you know what you want.

YOU DON'T HAVE TIME?

I don't have time for... I don't have time because I have to... I don't have time because... I don't have time for... I don't have time because...When I have time, I will... You know these kinds of excuses, don't you? I have heard them many times, but not because I work with a great number of people, but because I once used them myself. Honestly, even now, from time to time, they sneak into my mind. Now, however, I have enough power to bite my tongue whenever I am about to say something like that.

I agree with you that you are very busy - you have family, company, friends, and picnics, and I know that there are only 24 hours in a day. However, I do not agree with anybody, not even with myself, when I hear the excuse, "I don't have time." What happens when we say to ourselves, " I don't have time?" At that moment, we give our brain a clear order not to bother to do the task, because there is no time anyhow. With words, we affect our actions strongly. We will talk more about this in the chapter about emotions. I know that many of you can hardly wait to get to that chapter, but first we have to face the truth. Do you think that somebody who earns 10 times more also has 10 times more time in a day? Of course not, but that person is capable of organizing, specifying clear goals, setting up priorities and focusing on the results to be achieved.

NO, I DON'T HAVE TIME - I DON'T KNOW WHY

Two years ago, I noticed that I was slipping in the one area that largely determines how much energy I have for work and achievement. I'm talking about the field of healthy nutrition and recreation. There is a whole chapter devoted to that, because it is so very important. One day, I found myself breathless after walking up to my office on the second floor. It took me a few moments before I could talk again. My legs were shaking, and I had the feeling that I might fall. That did it! If I didn't start taking care of my health, all the money in the world would not help me, because I would not be around to spend it. Until that moment, I kept telling myself that I did not have time for recreation, because I was too busy. Since then, I devote two hours at least four to five times weekly to take care of my physical condition.

It is interesting; because I now run two companies, and I have twice the work and commitments compared to two years ago. The only difference is that I no longer use the excuse "I don't have time." I am simply aware that this is a precondition for success, happiness and contentment.

Soon, you reach the point where you have to stop and write down your dreams and goals. By now, you have probably realized the importance of goals for your success. However, I will still remind you: whether you think that you do not have time, or if you think that you do, it's all right. Do the exercise. We will soon get to the chapter on how to control your emotions, where you will be able to learn how to control your anger, fear, anxiety as well as your life and your happiness.

> "You are the only one who knows what you stand to gain or lose by not doing the exercise."
> Smiljan Mori

7 STEPS TOWARD SETTING UP ENTHUSIASTIC GOALS

When the year is coming to an end and the new one is on the doorstep, from which we expect much, we usually think about what we have achieved and what we would like to achieve in the new one. This is the time when we make small and big decisions and set new goals. Perhaps we think about how nice it would be if in the next year we would not have the same problems as we did in the past one. This is a year that we might like to forget.

> "If you use excuses wisely, you will be able to defend yourself well in the court of failure."
> Smiljan Mori

No matter what, the year is behind us, and we have to learn something from it. The worst thing would be just to forget it. So, now is the time for seven steps that will lead you to a better life in the New Year, or to a new life stage. I can assure you that you will make progress in every field of your life if you stick to the seven steps. This method of setting goals is not only useful at the

THE ART OF SETTING GOALS

end of the year; you can and should use it daily for setting goals or tasks in any field of your life. The majority of people really do set new goals at the end of the year, and they even make so-called NEW YEAR'S RESOLUTIONS that they never keep.

EXERCISE 18

STEP 1: WRITE DOWN PAST ACHIEVEMENTS

a) First, you have to find out precisely everything you achieved in the past year. Grab a pen and write down all the achievements, courageous acts, unusual events, all the loving feelings, and results in different areas. Note every bit of progress, every moment, which filled you with happiness, joy, delight, or cheerfulness. Remember everything that was fun or memorable in connection with family, friends or career. Let this become a New Year's treasure.

_____
_____
_____
_____
_____
_____
_____

b) Write down also everything that has hurt you in the past year. Write down the experiences that you wouldn't like to have again, the mistakes you must not repeat. Ask yourself how you can use all of that in the next year and what you can learn from all that. Acknowledge what you didn't enjoy and what confused you. Of course, write only about events which you are able to control. Don't write about those which you couldn't influence at all (like war or death of a family member or celebrity). Regarding these events, write down how you would react if they happened to you again. Learn from experience!

_____
_____
_____
_____
_____
_____
_____

c) In the past year, did you make any decision that improved your life, or will you do so in the next year (will you start a new business, a temporary job, stop smoking, start a healthy life, take exercise, meet new people or make friendships)?

_____
_____
_____
_____
_____
_____
_____

STEP 2: BECOME SELF-CONFIDENT

You have to gain confidence so that you can set inspiring goals. You can become self-confident by remembering all the things you achieved, the ones that used to be dreams, goals or wishes. We tend to remember only the bad things that happened to us. We remember the mistakes that we made. The goals, dreams or wishes we achieved or realized, we tend to take for granted.

Write down what you have today that used to be only a dream. Do not wait! If you have not started writing, do it now! Do not delay until tomorrow; it is important to take the first step now.

_____
_____
_____
_____
_____
_____
_____

Now, after you have written down all those wonderful things you have achieved in the past year, do the following exercise:

Circle the three achievements that were the most difficult to accomplish.

For each achievement, add a short comment (everything you had to do to get it). Maybe you had to be firm, self-confident and focused. Perhaps, to succeed, you went to a seminar, read a book, talked to a friend or acquaintance, or imitated somebody. After answering this question, you will find the pattern that makes you succeed. All you have to do is to use the same pattern next year. Most likely, you will succeed.

STEP 3: GET INSPIRED

For you to set new goals that will inspire you all year long, you have to get INSPIRED yourself. INSPIRATION=ENERGY. With enthusiasm, you can change invisible things into visible, dreams into reality.

You can do this in the following way:

Get yourself into top condition! That is the condition in which you can make decisions for the next year and create your ideal vision.

In ten minutes, write down everything you would like to achieve in the next year, the next five years, and the next decade. Do not set limitations; do not consider if it is possible. Write down what you would like to learn, try, experience or give. Write your financial goals, professional goals, and goals concerning your family; in other words, write down whatever comes to mind.

_____
_____
_____
_____
_____

STEP 4: BE SPECIFIC

You wrote what you would like to achieve in the coming years. Circle your four most important yearly goals. These are the goals which you would like to achieve in the next year. It is very important to know what is most important for YOU - not what is important for others.

STEP 5: REINFORCE YOURSELF

Now that you know your main goals, you must turn "I COULD HAVE" into "I HAVE TO." To change "I could have" into "I have to," you must have strong reasons. If you have strong enough reasons, you will find a way to achieve your goals. Beside each of these big four goals, write down why you wish to achieve them. The more reasons you have, the greater your motivation will be.

THE ART OF SETTING GOALS

Write:

What these goals will bring to you and what you are going to learn from the experience.

_____
_____
_____
_____

What will happen if you do not achieve them?

_____
_____
_____
_____

> "If you find out that failure is only a detour, you're well on the way to success."
> — Corrie Ten Boom

Sometimes, the fear of loss is bigger than the desire to earn. Use the method of the "dying person." Ask yourself, "When I'm on my deathbed, how will I feel about my life? What will I say to myself? What will I miss if I don't do this?" In this way, you will find out if you are ready to pay the price for success or failure.

STEP 6: KEEP THE INITIAL MOTIVATION

The easiest way to keep the initial motivation is to make two important decisions RIGHT NOW. I demonstrate at our seminars how important it is to make the decisions that can change your life. Which two decisions must you make first?

a) Make one small decision about what you are going to do now, maybe even today, and, with it, prove that you are serious about the next goal or goals for the next year. That is the small step. Do not underestimate the strength of something small, as seemingly insignificant actions can turn your life upside down. Four years ago, I decided that nobody else would make decisions about my career, promotions, earnings, happiness and vacations. That small decision allowed me to live a completely different, contented life.

b) Make one big decision, and decide on the one big move you will make, which will change your life.

> "If you're thinking about something, it is a dream. If you are talking about something, it is a vision. Only after you do something does it become reality."
>
> Smiljan Mori

It is important that you never set goals without taking steps for their realization. So do it now, without delay!

STEP 7: KEEP KEEPING TRACK OF YOUR GOALS

Most people keep track of their goals only at the end of the year. At that time, however, there is no further possibility of concentrating your energy in the right direction. If you keep checking on your goals and your progress at least monthly, you have more possibilities to achieve them. If you check them twice a month, you will achieve them for sure. It is even better if you find a coach to direct you and encourage you. Just as sportsmen need their personal coaches to get from them the best results and direct them, we, too, need a coach to help us achieve goals in both personal and professional areas.

THE ART OF SETTING GOALS

Once more, don't wait until tomorrow; start planning today and you will succeed!

At this moment, you do not need to consider whether certain goals are achievable or not, or if you have enough knowledge or skills. We will talk about these things in the chapter on emotions. The only things that hold you back from having everything you want are your subconscious fears, limiting beliefs and unnecessary doubt and worry. We will focus on getting rid of these in the chapter on emotions.

EXERCISE IN SETTING GOALS

EXERCISE 19

1. My goals in the area of personal and spiritual growth are:
(Write down everything that comes to your mind)

_____
_____
_____

1.a) My four most important goals in this area:

_____
_____
_____

1.b) Pain
   Of what will I be deprived if I don't achieve these goals - emotionally, financially, physically, and/or spiritually?

_____
_____
_____

1.c) Pleasure

What rewards will follow after achieving the goals - emotionally, financially, physically, and/or spiritually?

_____
_____
_____

2. My goals for personal health:
(Write down everything that comes to your mind.)

_____
_____
_____

2.a) My four most important goals in this area:

_____
_____
_____

2.b) Pain

Of what will I be deprived if I don't achieve these goals - emotionally, financially, physically, and/or spiritually?

_____
_____
_____

2.c) Pleasure

What rewards will follow after achieving this goal - emotionally, financially, physically, and/or spiritually?

_____
_____
_____

THE ART OF SETTING GOALS

3. My goals in my professional life:
(Write about everything that comes to your mind)

_____
_____
_____

3.a) My four most important goals in this area:

_____
_____
_____

3.b) Pain

    Of what will I be deprived if I don't achieve these goals - emotionally, financially, physically, and/or spiritually?

_____
_____
_____

3.c) Pleasure

    Which rewards will follow after achieving the goals - emotionally, financially, physically, and/or spiritually?

_____
_____
_____

4. My financial goals:
(Write down everything that comes to your mind)

_____
_____
_____

4.a) My four most important goals in this area are:

_____
_____
_____

4.b) Pain

Of what will I be deprived if I don't achieve these goals - emotionally, financially, physically, and/or spiritually?

_____
_____
_____

4.c) Pleasure

What rewards will follow after achieving these goals - emotionally, financially. physically, and/or spiritually?

_____
_____
_____

5. My material goals (houses, cottages, cars...):
(Write down everything that comes to mind.)

_____
_____
_____

5.a) My four most important goals in this area:

_____
_____
_____

5.b) Pain

Of what will I be deprived if I don't achieve these goals emotionally, financially, physically, and/or spiritually?

___

5.c) Pleasure

What rewards will follow after achieving these goals - emotionally, financially, physically, and/or spiritually?

___

7 WAYS TO MAINTAIN MOTIVATION FOR ACHIEVEMENT OF GOALS

1ST WAY: VISUALIZE YOUR GOALS

The most appropriate moment to visualize your goals is in the morning right after you wake up. Before you start, set your alarm clock to go off 15 minutes later because you may fall asleep during this exercise. The aim is to keep yourself awake so that you can visualize while your brain is still in the alpha phase*, that is, the condition of the brain when we are nearly sleeping or dreaming. Relax, close your eyes and follow the next steps:

- In your thoughts, count slowly from one hundred to zero. After each number, pause a second.
- When you get to zero, start to imagine yourself reaching a goal, or imagine the specific goals you want to achieve. Include all your organs of sense: smell, hearing, taste, and

touch. Allow your whole body to feel what it is like to reach the goal.
- Then keep repeating, "I am completely sure that I will achieve my goals!"
- Then tell yourself, "Now I will count from one to five. When I reach five, I will open my eyes, and I will feel absolutely relaxed. I will feel better than before."

2nd WAY: CONSOLIDATE YOUR GOALS

Write down your goals in big letters on sheets of paper (you can stick on a picture as well) and post these all over your living space. Since you can "see your goals" everywhere, you will keep remembering what motivates you and what you are living for.

3rd WAY: TALK ABOUT YOUR GOALS

A good way to focus on the achievement of your goals and to stay motivated so that your goals become part of your life is to entrust them to other people. They will be as thrilled that you plan to achieve these goals as you are. However, do not share your goals with somebody who will label you as an unrealistic dreamer! Find a friend who also wants to achieve goals, and help each other on the way.

> "We usually find that happy circumstances are the result of our doings."
> Oliver Goldsmith

*Jose Silva's Ultra-mind ESP systems Career Press, 200

4th WAY: LISTEN TO MOTIVATIONAL PROGRAMS, OR ATTEND MOTIVATIONAL SEMINARS

In this way, you will regain enthusiasm for your goals, develop new ones and get energy for work. Moreover, at these seminars, you will socialize with people who think as you do. One way to begin a very motivated day is the so-called motivational breakfast.

During the drive, listen to motivational tapes with topics that address your goals. No doubt it is better to listen to these than to negative news!

5th WAY: FIND YOURSELF A TUTOR

Find somebody who has already achieved what you would like to achieve, and who has sufficient knowledge to help you to realize your dreams, goals and wishes. Define a schedule to include when you meet him or her personally or over the phone. I, too, had a tutor and an excellent coach, Mr. Boris Vene (author of the international bestseller From the Diary of a Millionaire or Wealth Lies Within You). He directed me when I needed help. Until I found him, my tutors were books, or audio and videotapes.

6th WAY: WRITE YOUR GOALS ON SMALL CARDS

My colleague and friend, Kristijan, has a very good method of constant motivation for his goals. He writes down on small cards the most important goals that he wants to achieve in a year, in a month and in a day. He places them in his wallet, his car, and even in the folder he uses for sales meetings. Small cards like that can be very useful because you have them on hand every moment and can review them while, for example, waiting for a meeting or when you are stuck in a traffic jam. Using these cards is definitely better than getting angry at the frustrating things around you!

7th WAY: FORM A "WINNING TEAM"

Find four or five friends, colleagues or others who think as you do and who also have a strong drive to achieve their goals. Meet them regularly (weekly, monthly) to exchange experiences, knowledge, sources and assets for reaching the goals.

> *"Perseverance is failing nineteen times and succeeding the twentieth."*
> - Julie Andrews

What is Secret Number 3? Are you eager to learn more? Success is born with Secret Number 3. Let us find out what it is.

SECRET #3:

THE ROOTS OF MOTIVATION

EMOTIONS

"You can overcome fears if you grab them from the right side. Fear is an emotion. Emotions lie completely within ourselves and are only as strong as we allow them to be. The human race is gifted with intelligence. Intelligence (and not emotions) should be the leading force in our life, if we want to taste at least some happiness in this world. Emotions give color to life; without them, we would be pathetic creatures. But we have to control them; otherwise, they will control us. That goes especially for fear, which, if given free rein, will reduce all of us to trembling shadows of men, for whom only death can bring release."

John M. Wilson

IN THIS CHAPTER, YOU WILL DISCOVER:

How six basic human needs affect your life.

☙

How your thoughts affect the way you feel.

☙

How to overcome your doubts and fears forever.

☙

How to control your emotions, so that they do not control you and your destiny.

☙

How to discover the rooted beliefs and fears that are obstacles on your way to feeling excellent, and achieving good health and unlimited wealth.

☙

How to avoid the magic circle of failure.

☙

Which are the most important basic aspects for a wonderful life and to feel better.

☙

How, with the help of your body, you can change your emotions.

☙

How, with the help of positive words, you can release positive feelings.

☙

How to get rid of excess anxiety for good.

☙

Which techniques to use to overcome fears and phobias.

EMOTIONS

If you want to be very motivated and successful, you will have to be able to control your emotions effectively. Your emotions will control how you feel, and that will determine the quality of your actions and in turn, the results you can achieve.

Emotions are that area of the wheel of life that propels the whole wheel. You can have wonderful ideas, strategies and knowledge, but you are not going to be successful in your life if you cannot overcome your fears, doubts, negative emotions, frustrations and self-destructive beliefs. Your emotions have an impact on your characteristic attitude toward life, toward people, even toward yourself. They affect your attitude toward money and toward your work or career. Emotions make people cry or laugh, encourage or criticize, succeed or fail, be energetic or depressed, be angry or happy, optimistic or pessimistic, courageous or afraid.

Because of emotions, people hate or love each other, agree or disagree with each other, encourage or oppose, progress or regress. Because of emotions, companies succeed or fail. Because of emotions, businessmen dare to invest or not. Because of emotions, your children are going to be happy, successful and contented, or they will have problems. Emotions are the most delicate and yet the least researched field.

Despite being so important that they make the wheel of life revolve, we do not pay them enough attention, neither in the personal nor in the professional areas of life. Companies also do not pay enough attention to emotions. It is not a coincidence that in almost all companies, they ask me to teach them interpersonal communications - how management can better communicate with employees. That seems to be a problem all over, and it does reflect on client relationships, as well as on the progress of the company overall. All these kinds of problems are rooted in not knowing our emotional states and, consequently, ourselves.

Whenever a question about communications comes up, I always first talk about emotions. When employees understand their feelings, they will understand why they are reacting as they do. After understanding the causes, they will be able to get rid of the consequences of inefficient or negative communication.

In this chapter, I do not intend to write only about the methods of communication among people, but I will also touch on the most important part of communication: how to communicate with yourself. How you communicate with yourself will determine, to a great extent, how you are going to feel and what are you going to achieve in your life.

SATISFACTION OF BASIC HUMAN NEEDS

Before we go deeper into the area of emotions, which is one of the most important areas on the wheel of life, you should know why we behave as we do. Why do some people take drugs, drink alcohol, bite or cry? Why are they sick? Why do some people dye their hair? Everything we do, we do for a reason. With our actions, we try to satisfy one of our six human needs*. Although we all have the same needs, we satisfy them in different ways. For example, some people relax by lighting a cigarette, getting aggressive or taking drugs, while others read a book, exercise or listen to music. Ways of satisfying our needs are different and each of us chooses our own way. When we know which needs we satisfy with specific negative forms of behavior, we can design healthier ways for satisfying those needs. The power of a person lies in their ability to choose freely what specific things will mean in life.

*Abraham Maslow, a psychiatrist, who, in his late 40s, developed a hierarchical theory of human needs, i.e. pyramid of needs by Maslow.

1. NEED FOR SECURITY/COMFORT

Our need for comfort and to avoid pain can be satisfied in negative, neutral and positive ways. It is important for survival. If a person does not feel basic security, he or she cannot even function. Have you ever felt uncertain about work, salary, money, examinations or your career? Because we are different, we try to satisfy the need for security in different ways. We all need a basic sense of security, regardless of our religion, race, sex, creed, beliefs or education. Some satisfy the need for security by doing the same things at the same time and in an accustomed way every day. Some, for this purpose, surround themselves with people who are smarter and better than they are, and feel they are able to control things in this way. Others try to control everybody around them to satisfy this need. Some are very religious. Others smoke, drink or overeat.

> "When people are made to feel secure and important and appreciated, it will no longer be necessary for them to whittle down others in order to seem bigger in comparison."
> Virginia Arcastle

Each of us satisfies our needs in our own way. The only question is whether that way is destructive or inspiring to you, and if it helps you. If you use drugs or alcohol, watch TV or procrastinate actions in order to be safe, these are destructive ways of satisfying your needs. However, you may feel safe in knowing that you can find a way - even a destructive way - to feel secure in any situation. That means that your identity gives you security. You feel safe because you know that in any situation you can find the solution to satisfy your needs.

The next point is very interesting: when you become absolutely certain about something, (for example, in a relationship when you know exactly what will happen, where it will happen, what you will feel) suddenly, you become bored. A lot of people think that the art of life is to get so much money that you do not need to work anymore. However, in fact, the life of such people looks like a big desert. Emotions slowly lose their power. Because of that, they try to create an oasis from a desert - with a new preoccupation involving alcohol, drugs or food.

WAYS OF SATISFYING THE NEED FOR SECURITY

Positive - productive ways:

- learning
- developing self-confidence

Negative - unproductive ways:

- overeating
- controlling others
- helplessness
- negative identity
- jealousy
- aggression

2. NEED FOR DISTINCTION/ BEING DIFFERENT

This is a need for:

- surprise
- diversity
- challenges
- distinction
- uncertainty
- tension
- excitement

In our lives, we need events and things that allow us to grow. If everything develops monotonously and comes predictably, we do not grow because we do not need to. But if we are not certain about something, we have to grow in order to control that sense of uncertainty.

We can satisfy this need with drinking coffee, shopping, going to movies or traveling. Watching movies is interesting because, on the one hand, it does excite us, while on the other, it gives us sensations of security (we feel safe because we know that we are not going to die, but the actor in the picture will). Is there any movie you have seen many times? Why did you watch it so many times? It may be because, in one way, you feel safe knowing what's going to happen in the movie; on the other hand, you hope that you will have forgotten some details from it in order to satisfy the need for uncertainty. The needs for security and diversity are opposite, but if you want to feel good, you have to fulfill both needs.

WAYS OF SATISFYING THIS NEED:

Positive and productive ways:

- new adventures
- new apartment
- accepting new challenges
- new knowledge

Negative - unproductive ways:

- alcohol
- drugs
- changing your job
- cheating

The need for security and the need for diversity are contradictory

3. NEED FOR IMPORTANCE

This concerns the sensation that we are:

- important
- needed
- that our lives have meaning
- clever
- unique

The need for importance can be satisfied by being violent. This way is very common in our society. Why? The explanation is very simple: if somebody has no education, are poor, and suddenly they put a gun to your head, they become very important. For this, they do not need education or reputation. With this kind of behavior, people can satisfy a few needs simultaneously; suddenly, they become important; they get a sense of security by controlling the situation, and, at the same time, they satisfy the need for diversity, because what they are doing is a very uncommon experience. This way of satisfying needs does not require any education at all.

> "It's nice to be important but it's nicer to be kind."
> John M. Templeton

You can get the same effect – feeling important - in other, more productive and healthier ways. Here are some suggestions: possess knowledge that others do not, continuously educate yourself, dress uniquely, get a unique hairdo, get a tattoo, or buy special things (such as a house or car that nobody else has). Each of us has to satisfy this need to feel important. The only question is in which way we will satisfy it. People quarrel among themselves to prove who is more important. You can also be of importance by giving love, attention and money to others. Each of us has a different way of satisfying these needs.

WAYS OF SATISFYING THE NEED TO FEEL IMPORTANT:

Positive - productive ways:

- getting titles (PhD., honorary degree, graduate degree)
- getting acknowledgments
- constant personal growth

- having children
- possessing material things
- dressing in style
- outstanding cars

Negative - unproductive ways:

- disregarding others
- illness (as a reason for getting attention)
- constant complaints
- aggression toward others and ourselves
- fights
- violence

If you wish to be important, you have to be unique or different from others. This is in contradiction with the next human need.

4. NEED TO BE ATTACHED/ LOVE

- desire for intimacy
- to feel a connection
- to be a part of a group
- to be with somebody

Some people, especially those who wish to fulfill their need for importance and who succeed in satisfying their drive to become very famous, often fall into conflict situations. Suddenly, they are left alone. They are afraid of satisfying their need to be attached, because they are haunted by the idea that somebody only wants to be with them to get something from them. It is hard to find a partner because they are of the belief that they are wanted only because of their money. In contrast, some people feel loved by their partners, but eventually, because of that love lose their identity. He or she starts to ask: what about me? How can I be special and important? That is the reason why many marriages fail.

Becoming sick from time to time can also satisfy the need to feel important. Suddenly, you have many visitors; people feel sorry for you, and they are compassionate towards you. Under normal circumstances, this does not happen. Even if you were lying on the street, most people would pass you by. You can also satisfy this need by causing problems for others. For example, children, when they do not get your attention, will start annoying you and cause problems only in order to see that you care about them. This is true not only for children but also for adults.

WAYS TO SATISFY THE NEED FOR ATTACHMENT/LOVE

Positive - productive ways:

- spirituality
- attachment to nature
- sex
- art
- music
- memberships in clubs

Negative - unproductive ways:

- hypochondria
- bad relationships (friends, family)
- smoking, alcohol, drugs

5. NEED TO GROW AND DEVELOP

Many people, despite financial success, are very unhappy because they never satisfy the need for personal growth and the need for development.

Your need for security can be satisfied by having control over those around you. To get attention, many people feel the need for escape with drugs, the need for importance by disregarding others, the need for attachments with constant problems that others have to solve. In all these cases, people pay attention to you, and you feel loved. Yet I have to warn you about something very important: if you try to satisfy your needs in these ways, you are not going to be satisfied. You will be contented only when you find positive ways to satisfy your needs. You must find ways that will spark and contribute to your personal growth. You are already one-step closer by reading this book.

It does not matter how much you earn, what kind of car you drive, or what nice people think of you. If you do not feel that you are growing personally, you are never going to be content. If you do not grow, you start to die within yourself, inside of you. When somebody commits suicide, we ask ourselves, "How could he or she do that?" Of course, there can many reasons; usually, one of them is that there was no growth, no personal development.

6. NEED TO CONTRIBUTE

If you truly want to be happy, then you have to grow and contribute, otherwise you fall into a comfort zone. Some time ago, I found my way to grow and contribute. You have to find your own. If you help others to be happy, you will be happy too. Remember that you always have to give other people what you would like to receive. Never do to somebody what you would not like somebody to do to you. Each of us can satisfy at any time any of our needs, no matter what is going on around us. You have to ask yourself the following question, "What would I have to do or believe, what significance would I have to place on something, in order to get more satisfaction in this area of my life?"

Now that you know why people behave in different ways, I invite you to read on and learn the next secret of motivation.

AS YOU THINK, SO DO YOU FEEL

In this chapter, you will discover some simple but effective ideas that will cause a real revolution in your life:

1. You feel in the same way that you think. Your way of thinking will determine your feelings. You will discover that some negative emotions like depression, anger, fear and anxiety are not the result or consequence of negative events that happened to you, but depend on how you think about them and what significance you give to them.

2. Most negative emotions come from illogical thoughts (destructive, diverted thinking).

3. You will find out things that affect your feelings, i.e. emotions derived from the following:

a) physiology of the body (pose, facial expressions, gestures, breathing, muscle tone)
b) the words we say
c) thoughts, beliefs

4. You have the strength and ability to change your feelings in a second, but only if you want to.

When you are upset, you probably think about negative things that happened to you. You might feel angry or frightened because you lost your job or because somebody you love has criticized or rejected you. It is almost natural to feel miserable when something goes wrong or something bad happens to you.

Try to imagine a moment when you were sad, frightened, worried or angry. Maybe something similar has happened to you recently. Describe what happened. Be very precise. Who were you with? What happened? When? Where were you?

Now describe how you felt. Examine the table on the following page, and use it to clarify what you felt. Check the negative feelings on the left that best described the state you were in at the time. Then choose the word(s) on the right that best describe your feelings in that moment. Try to pick an event that triggered in you a specific negative emotion.

I was angry because of:

EMOTION	WORDS WHICH EXPRESS FEELINGS
ANGER	furious, crazy, mad, vengeful, sensitive, excited, wild, irritated, enraged,
NERVOUSNESS	worried, excited, nervous, panicky, frightened, uncomfortable, edgy, terrified
HUMILIATION/ CONFUSION	stupid, ridiculous, foolish, a laughing stock, helpless, confused
GUILT	humiliated, guilty, ashamed, bad, ugly, a loser, doubtful,
DESPERATION	pessimistic, frightened, fearful, opposed, terrified
LONELINES	alone, forgotten, abandoned, rejected, neglected
STRESS	overworked, overcharged, under pressure, burnt out, exhausted, fatigued, tense, overloaded

Do you know what causes negative emotions? Some people think that they get upset because bad things are happening to them. It may be that a loved one has hurt you or friends let you down. It is normal for us to feel hurt or angry when somebody we trust betrays or hurts us. Sometimes, despite everything, that happens; it is hard to keep a positive attitude towards the person who hurt us, or towards the event, and at the same time keep our self-respect. Has this ever happened to you?

Did somebody ever abuse your trust and were you insulted because of that?

Some people believe that they become depressed for other reasons.

They feel abandoned and unworthy, and they think that there is something very wrong with them. They tell themselves that they are not self-confident, or are not sufficiently charming, beautiful or smart to be happy or worth something "more" in their lives. They compare themselves with others who appear to be more self-confident and successful. Then, they just decide, "I'm not like that. How can I be happy at all? I'm just a second-class citizen, a born loser." Do you sometimes think about yourself like that?

Finally, some people become depressed because of problems they have in their professional lives or in relationships. Many of us connect self-respect with success at work and in relationships with others, such as those in our community. When we lose a job or somebody rejects us, we are desperate. Have you had such an experience of rejection?

All of this is correct to a certain extent. But all these assumptions make one big mistake: they want to make you into a victim of circumstances over which you have no control. No matter how strong the pill you take, it still cannot protect you from things that happen from time to time. There are few of us who can avoid trouble and disappointment in our lives. That is a simple fact that you have to face.

I will tell you a simple but revolutionary way in which you can control your feelings. The idea is not new, and you, too, have the capability within you to use this technique. The famous Greek philosopher, Epictetus, said, "A man isn't worried because of one thing, but because of the way he looks upon it or on certain events." That simply means that your thoughts are under the control of your feelings and not events.

SEPTEMBER 11, 2001

I was in Hawaii at one of the seminars given by Anthony Robbins (an expert in the psychology of change and personal achievement and author of the book, Awaken the Giant Within). There were more than 2000 people from 80 countries present. There were people of all nationalities and religions. The seminar was going on at the time of the terrorist attack on the WTC. Among the participants, there was a young woman who had come against the wishes of her fiancé. The fiancé threatened never to marry her if she attended the seminar. She replied that she wasn't sure if he was "Mister Right," and it would be better for her to go to the seminar to find out within herself if he were the right one or not. After a few days of intensive work on herself, she concluded that he was the perfect man for her. She found out that she had to change a few things in herself. On Monday night, she decided to call him at work and let him know that she loved him, and that they could marry after she returned from the seminar. Because he did not answer the phone, she left a message.

The next morning, he called her from an office situated almost on the top of one of the WTC towers. The tower had just been hit by a plane. He told her that he did not know what had happened, but it was dark and there was smoke everywhere, and he said he thought he would die. Just before he hung up, he wished her happiness in her life. Can you imagine what happened in the hall when this woman stood up and told her story? An ex-boyfriend had been killed in a traffic accident, and now this had happened, but she was standing in front of everybody brave and courageous. She was crying, but she did not say that her life was over, as most people would have done. She was hurt, but the pain gave her strength to live. She will dedicate her life to helping others to overcome even the worst crises, like the one she came through. Instead of labeling the event with only a negative meaning, she found something positive in it for herself.

This is yet more proof that the most important thing is what significance you give to any event that happens to you.

> "He who loses wealth loses much; he who loses a friend loses more; but he that loses his courage loses all."
> - Miguel De Cervantes

You might say that the story sounds very American, but I tell it because it actually happened there. It was interesting to watch and listen to the participants at the seminar. Each person found a different significance in the event. I was in the fitness center when events began to unfold. I only really heard about the event just before the planned beginning of the seminar that day. My first reaction was very different from that of the 70 participants in the seminar who had companies and employees in both WTC towers. I was terribly shocked and hurt, naturally, but I was also concerned about how and when I'd get home if all the airports closed.

We are always afraid of something. What is important is that this fear, or any other emotion, does not stop us from moving forward. Once again, we get upset because of the way we think about certain events, things or persons.

Next example: You lost a job or experienced some other rejection. Of course, you are going to be sad and critical of yourself because you are going to repeat that you are not good enough. You may think, "Something must be wrong with me." Maybe you will be nervous or angry, and, in this case, you will say to yourself, "Life isn't fair. Why is this always happening to me?" These kinds of negative thoughts are normal and natural. Almost everybody thinks that way sometimes. Only later will you learn to change these kinds of thoughts so you can change your feelings.

EXERCISE 20

Take the last example of something that made you angry. Ask yourself, "What was I thinking when I got upset? What did I say when I felt insulted, angry and worried?" In the first balloon, write down your negative thoughts and in the other what you were telling yourself.

By now, you must have realized that your emotions and feelings depend more on the way you think than on what really happens to you.

How is it possible that we have so many different ways of feeling? It is because specific emotions are the result of specific ways of thinking.

Let us take a very simple case.

Suppose you catch a cold and then influenza. You are angry, nervous and you tell yourself, "This isn't fair at all! I am too busy for this nonsense. My work is going to suffer again. In addition, it is happening when I have to finish this important project!"

Alternatively, you can think in this way, "I'm not surprised because lately I really have been working beyond my capabilities. I have not exercised for a long time. I will have to find a balance between my work and my private life. Now is the time to lie down a little, read a book and recuperate for new ventures. The world won't collapse if I have to lie down for a while."

In both cases, the end of the story will be the same; you will have to stay in bed and recover. Only your emotions will be very different. It all depends on how you think about it.

This idea is very important, but I know you may not agree with me completely. You still might think that other people or strange circumstances can upset you or make you angry, no matter how you think. I can understand your reservations.

Allow me to ask you a question, "How do you feel right now after reading these lines? Are you skeptical?" If that is the case, you have probably been shaking your head and telling yourself that my arguments have not convinced you.

Are you angry? If you are, you are probably telling yourself that Smiljan Mori is just a "lot of hot air" and that he wrote this book only for profit. Are you sad and frightened? If you feel like that, then you can be sure that the techniques and methods described are not going to help you. Of course, I do not believe everything I read either. You can have doubts, but have them with an open mind. When I started to read this kind of thing and later to use it, some of the techniques worked, and some did not. I told myself that if it helped somebody else, it might help me too. Of course, it is best if somebody demonstrates it to you in practice. We do that at the seminars where people experience big changes in a short period. It is interesting that people may already have the knowledge and tools to change within themselves, but still need somebody to show them how to do it and to keep reminding them over and over.

Do you feel excited, happy and full of hope? If you do, then this book can change your life for the better and also help you to a better and a more contented life.

You are all reading the same book, but each of you will have different feelings. Do you know why? It is not the words that cause ten distinct feelings in ten different people. If the words written in these pages do not determine your feelings, then you must have been creating your own feelings. Do you understand what am I saying? Your thoughts, not events determine your temperament.

Look at the table on the next page. On the left-hand side, are listed different emotions. Write down in the first column specific events that trigger these emotions. Write down in the second column thoughts that you connect with different types of emotions. In the third column, write down positive thoughts that can change your negative emotions towards these events.

The first two emotions in the table are SADNESS and DEPRESSION. Remember a moment when you were depressed or sad. What happened to you? What were you thinking about? If you felt sad and depressed, you were probably thinking about somebody or something you lost; perhaps you just lost a particular sensation in your mind. Has it ever happened that you were in a good mood, and then suddenly became sad, angry or depressed? Why? Think!

YOUR THOUGHTS AND YOUR EMOTIONS

EXERCISE 21

EMOTIONS	THOUGHTS	POSITIVE THOUGHTS
SADNESS AND DEPRESSION		
GUILT AND SHAME		
DISAPPOINTMENT		
ANGER		
ANXIETY, WORRY, FEAR, PANIC		
LONELINESS		
DESPERATION AND DISAPPROVAL		

EXERCISE 22

In the first column, write down events that can cause you to feel positive emotions. If you have not experienced any, make them up. Ask yourself, what could happen to me to feel all these positive emotions? In the second column, write down different ways in which you can experience all these positive emotions. These can be small actions, like seeing a movie, traveling, taking a stroll, singing or dancing. Count as many you can, because with positive actions you can break the pattern of negative emotions. Whenever any negative emotion occurs, think of the positive emotion you would like to feel instead, and then do something from the second column that will trigger them.

POSITIVE EMOTIONS	WAYS TO EXPERIENCE THESE
LOVE AND WARMTH	
GRATITUDE	
CURIOSITY	
EXCITEMENT AND PASSION	
FIRMNESS	
SELF-CONFIDENCE	
FLEXIBILITY	

CHEERFULNESS PLAYFULNESS	
HAPPINESS	
CONTRIBUTION	
JOY	
TRUST	
POWER	
COURAGE	

LET US NOT BE ANGRY WITH PEOPLE. LET US GET ANGRY AT OUR MEMORIES AND PICTURES FROM THE PAST

One Saturday morning, I was going to collect the watches we present to reward our successful workers at the beginning of the seminars. While I was driving, my girlfriend called me. She asked when we could meet for lunch. We exchanged some kind and loving words. The next question was, where was I going? That upset me. I answered that she should not be asking me such foolish questions. I hung up. Of course, I felt sorry immediately, but instead of apologizing to her, I asked myself why I reacted that way. What drove me to get so upset with her, although we had just had a pleasant conversation? I asked myself what I was thinking at the moment when I got angry, what I was telling myself, and what images were in my mind at the time? I concluded that I was not upset with her, but with an event from the past, which brought feelings of anger. I simply did not want to explain to her why I had to go for the watches right now. Her question reminded me of an event from the past that caused me pain and which I did not want to talk about. Instead of apologizing to her, I taped my thoughts for her to listen to later. I asked her what she was thinking when she experienced my outburst of anger. She told me that she felt guilty because she had obviously done something wrong, but she did not know what it was. Her feelings, too, came from her past, when her parents would tell her with raised voices that she had done something stupid. However, in principle, it was not my reaction that caused her to feel guilty; it was merely the memory of a similar event from the past.

As you can see, our reactions were determined by experiences from the past and not by specific events.

FEAR: THE VIRUS OF SUCCESS

Fear of failure is one of the biggest fears that prevents the majority of people from achieving in their lives what they really want and deserve. Fear is that limiting factor which can truly destroy your life. That is why it is good to know that you learned all these fears; you were not born with them. Similarly, you were not born with limiting beliefs - you have learned them. Research has shown that by the age of two, 50% of what you know about yourself and your capabilities has already been formed. By age six, 60%, by age eight, 80% of what you believe about your capabilities has already been learned. When you celebrate your 14th birthday, you have already formed 99% of the belief base of your capabilities and your potential*. This news is not very cheerful! However, you have to know that you were not born with limiting beliefs, but just thought you were. In the same way you acquired these limiting beliefs, you can dispose of them.

> **"Fear is the shadow of ignorance."**
> Eric Butterworth
>
> **"Fear is the lengthened shadow of ignorance."**
> - Arnold Glasgow

We will always be afraid of something. It is important that fear or any other emotion will not hold us back forever. We get upset over the way we think about certain events, things or persons.

When I tell people that they can have everything in life that they want, they just need to deal with their fears and limiting beliefs, they usually ask, "Really? How?"

---

*Rod Hall: 7 Strategies of Success, Tomorrow, Inc.; 2000

EMOTIONS

> "Three qualities define a real man. Honesty (saves him from anxiety), wisdom (saves him from doubt), courage (saves him from fear)."
> - Confucius

It is true. FEAR you can change into COURAGE in a second and change your weakness into strength. How this occurs, you will find out later. There is a simple way to change things that are obstacles in your quest to use all your potential.

The damage that is caused because of fears and limiting beliefs is enormous, but too many are not aware of it.

Let us review the most common fears that people face in their lives.

They are afraid of failure, afraid of asking questions, afraid of new jobs, afraid of the future; they are afraid of making a mistake; afraid to confess that they've got a problem; they are afraid of diseases; some are even afraid of success; they are afraid of being responsible for problems and failure in the company. Moreover, they are afraid of trying something new, of investing money in new projects, afraid of losing loved ones, of sickness, of change; they are afraid of what others might think of them.

FEAR OF TRUTH

At one of the presentations for our motivational seminar, I asked people what sorts of fears they experienced. One woman told me that her biggest fear was of the truth. We are afraid of hearing the truth about ourselves, about our behavior or position. It is true that we do not want to see the truth, which sometimes can hurt, even though it would be better to confess it to ourselves, because we would then progress more easily in our lives. Just as with hearing the truth about ourselves, many of us are afraid of telling other people the truth. We are afraid that we might hurt their feelings if we tell them what we really should.

FEAR OF COMPETITION

We are also very afraid of competition. A lot of mental energy is wasted thinking about what and how the competition is doing, instead of focusing on our own work and ourselves. Some time ago, I was to give a speech in front of representatives of a network marketing company. I was invited by a manager. He thought my speech would be a pleasant surprise for the leading workers. It was a surprise - but not a positive one! Some workers were scared that I would try to recruit, or "poach" their employees, so they were mistrustful of me from the beginning. Whatever their reasons were for behaving as they did, I learned a lot from that experience. I knew that I had higher and nobler intentions than recruiting people for my own business. My intentions and mission were to encourage more people to grow personally so that they could successfully realize the goals they had set up. I know that I am familiar with the techniques and strategies, which will allow them to achieve all of that faster than on their own.

WHAT IS COMPETITION FOR ONE PERSON IS WELCOME KNOWLEDGE FOR ANOTHER

It was a completely different picture when I was teaching insurance agents from a Slovene insurance company. Their manager was delighted that I was willing to share unselfishly my knowledge with others, even though the company was a competitor of ours. In my life, there is one leading proverb, "What you give you get; what you sow you reap!"

> "Fear of failure brings us to exactly where we don't want to be."
> Smiljan Mori

Moreover, I try to stick to the motto, "Do unto others what you would like to have done unto you." That has often given cause for thought.

HOW WE CAN GET RID OF ELEVEN YEAR-OLD FEARS WITHIN AN HOUR AND A HALF

In my work with people, I have met those with other kinds of fears; I could call these phobias, or an irrational fear of a specific thing or situation. I have worked with people who have been living for over 11 years in fear of open spaces, and who never left their home by themselves; they were afraid of snakes, of driving in the car or a plane, or of something else. For many years, they fought phobias; they tried therapists and psychiatrists, but in vain. When they did not see any solution anymore, they started taking pills, which did not remove the cause of the fear. For a long time now, I have been curious to see how quickly and efficiently you can remove something that people have fought for a very long time. That led me to techniques that can change people with almost "ultrasonic" speed. These are Richard Bandler's techniques of Neuro-Associative Conditioning, and the techniques of Neuro-associative training of Anthony Robbins and Erickson. I have tried these techniques myself, and found that they do work; I also started hypnotherapy and Gestalt therapy. I tested these techniques in order to appear on radio stations in Slovenia to talk about how to rid people of serious fears and limiting beliefs in a very short time.

> "When you overcome the rapids and avoid all the whirlpools and rocks, you will reach the ocean of pleasure and a happier, more pleasant and more successful life."
>
> Smiljan Mori

One year ago, I worked with Ana, a pleasant, middle-aged woman. I had known her for a year, but did not know about her problems. She hid them very well. One day, I met her on the staircase in my office building, and she was in a very bad mood. I asked her what was wrong. Of course, she said nothing, but I could see from her body language and facial expression (which you will read about shortly) that this was not true, so I persisted. She told me that she felt helpless - she was afraid to walk around by herself, and that she could not go anywhere without her husband or friends. She was fed up with lying, because nobody besides her husband knew about her problem. She had gone to therapists and psychotherapists for eleven years, but nothing helped. After a while, we met in my office for "therapy." After an hour and a half of consultation, Ana proudly walked out at 9.30 p.m. by herself on the streets. Of course, I waited for her to return. She was crying. She never thought that she would walk by herself again through the town, visit shops or drive her children to school. It was a pleasure to hear her words, "I cannot believe it; I spent only an hour and a half with you, after not being able to get rid of this problem for eleven years. I was already thinking of admitting myself to an institution so nobody would bother me ever again to go out with them for a drink or to a party."

NO MORE HAIR PULLING

At a motivational seminar in a high school, I met a student who had been pulling out her hair for ten years. All this time, she had been visiting therapists and psychotherapists, but they did not know how to help her. My therapy with her lasted 30 minutes and since then seven months have passed without any hair pulling. How can this kind of change happen in such a short time? With the help of techniques that I will describe later, soon I could identify the strong emotional event that triggered the habit. Then, I used the technique for sudden interruption of a thinking pattern and of negative actions, and then taught her how to substitute positive behavior for her old habits the next time she next finds herself in a stressful situation.

THAT WAS THE DAY I WAS REBORN

You can imagine what kind of power I gained when I managed to achieve the result just described. I said to myself, "I have to show this to people!" All over Slovenia, I started to hold lectures about how people can change their lives within an hour or a day if they wish. People are hungry for this kind of knowledge and so the first seminar was attended by numerous participants, the majority of whom, consequently, used the techniques and began to live better.

Why are people afraid? Why don't they want to change? It is because they are afraid of unknown territory. Most prefer to keep "the status quo" because they feel safer that way. Fears can help us to make wise decisions, but in this book, we talk about the kind of fears that can cause uncertainty, self-indulgence and unproductive acts, effectively hindering the way to success.

THE THREE AGENTS OF EMOTIONS

We feel because of three basic agents:

1. PHYSIOLOGY OF OUR BODY - PHYSIOLOGICAL CONTENT OF EMOTIONS

This involves the way we use our bodies, how we stand or sit, the state of our muscles (tense or relaxed), our hand gestures, the speed of our movements, breathing (slow or fast), facial expressions, where we focus our eyes (on the floor or upward). With changes in the physiology of the body, you can shift in a few seconds from one condition to another. I sincerely hope that you are doing the exercises described in the book, because only in this way will you see that things are really working. Many people know a lot but they never actually do anything. And these people usually say, "Oh, I know that already." It is not a question of whether you know it or not, but the question is whether you are acting on what you know. This book and all the seminars are directed toward action. What are you waiting for? Are you up for it?

EXERCISE 23

1. Stand in the position you take when you are depressed, sad and blue and completely without energy.

    Pay attention to the position of arms, legs, shoulders and head, where your eyes are turned, and how you breathe.

2. Stand up in the position you take when you are self-confident, sure of yourself, optimistic and full of energy.

Do you notice the difference in the physiological components of an excellent mood?

Now, repeat this exercise a few times in a row, so you can switch rapidly from a depressive to a self-confident mood and back. In that way, you will recognize that you can have an impact on your mood with the position of your body and with the expression on your face.

Do you remember Lidija from the beginning of the book? When I was doing therapy with her, she started an abnormal trembling when I asked why she was depressed. I wanted her to stop trembling, but she told me that she could not.

Then I asked her to get up immediately. Guess what happened? She calmed down in a moment. Everything changed when she altered the position and stance of her body. You also have such power. Thus, you can control your feelings, and you do not need to be depressed, nervous, anxious or angry. At our motivational seminars, the participants do the exercise, so that by the time they leave they are able to control their feelings.

> "A well-chosen word has often sufficed to stop a flying army, to change defeat into victory, and to save an empire."
> — Emile De Girardin

2. VERBAL COMPONENT OF EMOTIONS

These are the words you use to describe certain physical conditions and moods. These are the hypnotic sentences with which you influence subconsciously your mood, emotions and actions.

They are questions that you ask daily, and parables with which you describe your perception of the outer world and reflect your thoughts and feelings.

WORDS OF SUCCESS

Try to envision a person who is very successful on a professional level. How does he express himself? Which words does he use to describe his feelings and view of life in general? If you ask him, "How are you?" will he say, "Oh, so, so, I'm hanging in there; It's going to be better; I've been better; You see how the weather is..." or does he use strongly inflected words like, "wonderful", "fantastic" and "it's getting better." Remember what you say is what you feel; what you feel, you believe; what you believe becomes your belief; your beliefs influence your actions, and your actions are the results which you will achieve.

The words you speak trigger specific mental pictures that afterwards trigger specific emotions, and these determine your mood all day. What words do you use during the day, which make you feel bad?

> "A powerful agent is the right word. Whenever we come upon one of those intensely right words in a book or a newspaper, the resulting effect is as physical as it is spiritual...."
> Mark Twain

Perform the next exercise so that you will become aware of the strength of the words you are using.

EXERCISE 24

1. Repeat loudly the following sentence, "I'm not nervous!" Repeat that five times with stronger emotional intensity each time. How do you feel? You must have become slightly nervous. Why? Your brain cannot distinguish between "I am" and "I am not"; it just distinguishes emotionally colored words. How were you using your body while saying these words?

2. Now keep repeating, "I'm happy; I'm happy; I'm happy." The stronger the intensity you use, the more you will feel it, and then believe it, and your actions will be different than if you had used words with a negative emotional charge.

In the next few days, pay attention to your VOCABULARY OF SUCCESS.

When do you feel better?, if you are saying that you are overwhelmed, or if you are saying that you have to prioritize?

THE MIRACULOUS POWER OF METAPHORS

At a presentation for a motivational seminar in Zagorje, I was explaining the power of words and the influence of physiology on human emotions. One man said he believed all of that, but it was very hard to stay positive when you knew that "the bombs" were going to drop at work tomorrow. I asked him "What if you said, How can you remain upbeat if you knew that "daisies'" would fall at work tomorrow?" When he repeated this sentence after me, just the change of the word bomb into daisy made him smile. Both the physiology of his body and his facial expression changed.

> "The metaphor is perhaps one of man's most fruitful potentialities. Its efficacy verges on magic, and it seems a tool for creation which God forgot inside one of his creatures when He made him."
> Jose Ortega Y. Gasset

The words and the metaphors that we say aloud have incredible power. They can hurt or heal, bring hope or despair.

> "Words form the thread on which we string our experiences."
> Aldous Huxley

Franci, a very successful businessman from Ljubljana, told me during personal counseling that he could no longer stand the pressure at work, because he had a feeling that a sword was hanging above his head. When I told him to close his eyes and describe this sword to me, he described exactly at which height it hung, how big it was, how sharp it was, its color and even that it was moving closer to his head. Close your eyes for a moment and imagine that over your head is hanging a very sharp, shining, two-meter long sword that is about to fall on your head. How do you feel? How did Franci feel, even sleeping with a sword like that over his head? Not very pleasant, I believe. I suggested Franci to use a rather different metaphor or image. His new image was, "I have so many flowers to pick at work that I don't know whether should I pick the tulips or the daisies first." Wow! After a few months, I saw him again and his face was shining with a smile. Only then were we able to make progress in his professional and private life.

EMOTIONS

EXERCISE 25

Which metaphors are you using? Finish the following sentences.

Life is... _____

Money is..._____

I am a person who..._____

If your images and metaphors are negative, now is the right time to exchange them for positive ones and to keep repeating them until they become part of your vocabulary.

An example of a negative thought	An example of a positive thought
Life is a big ordeal	Life is a dance
Life is one big denial	Life is recognizing new things
Love can ruin you	Love is one of the most beautiful things you can give and get
I am at the bottom	I am preparing to rise again
I fell to the ground	I want to get up and run

I suggest that you take the 30-day mental challenge. It takes that long to change your habits—good or bad. If you want to get used to something, you have to practice it, and when you practice something, you get used to it.

THE POWER OF QUESTIONS

The questions we ask ourselves every day have a major influence on our feelings and our actions. At one of the seminars of Anthony Robbins in Hawaii, I met Gerald Coffee, or Jerry to his friends. Jerry was imprisoned for seven years in a cell no longer than two meters and not wider than a meter during the Vietnam War. Every day, he was hungry and thirsty and did not know what was happening to his family back home. Despite the horrible things that were happening to him, he didn't ask himself, "O God what have you done to me? My life is over." He asked himself better questions.

> "...It is only with the heart that one sees rightly; what is essential is invisible to the eye."
> Antoine De Saint-Exupery

His most powerful question was, "How can I use what happened to me to improve the lives of others?" After he emerged from imprisonment, he started to lecture, with friends, all over the world about the power that primary questions have in the lives of people. Since then, he has lectured about positive ways of thinking to more than ten thousand people. One of his friends from prison committed suicide; the other became an alcoholic. Why? Because both asked themselves very different primary questions.

WHAT IS YOUR PRIMARY QUESTION?

Lidija, who had tried to commit suicide twice in three months, was asked to identify the primary question she asked herself every day. It isn't necessary that you consciously ask yourself primary questions. They can appear inaudibly in your subconscious and affect your thinking and actions.

Lidija's primary question was, "Why is all of this happening to me? Why me? My life has no meaning anymore." No wonder she was thinking of committing suicide. In that way, she would easily avoid the pain she experienced in her childhood.

I helped Lidija to change her primary question into, "O God, thank you for the love and all the experiences you have given me. How can I share my experiences, knowledge and love with others?" With that question, the meaning of her life has changed.

Here are some examples of other primary questions of people I meet at my seminars and in personal counseling:

NEGATIVE PRIMARY QUESTIONS:

- What will others say about what I am doing now?
- What if I can't succeed?
- Will they reject me?
- How can I unconditionally please everybody around me?
- How can I ever be the best at what am I doing?
- How can I finish the task without mistakes?

POSITIVE PRIMARY QUESTIONS

- How can I be sure at this moment that I am doing the right things?
- How am I going to celebrate when I succeed?
- How many times will I succeed?

- How can I share my love and attention among people who want it?
- How can I give everything from myself and be happy with every sign of progress?

Do you see the difference between the first and second set of questions? It is rather big, isn't it? If you choose the second ones, you will be much less miserable than if you choose the negative ones.

What are YOUR primary questions, which constantly arouse in you negative feelings, and that you would like to get rid of? Write them down and turn them into questions that will inspire you and give you power and positive energy.

OH NO! WHAT IF SOMETHING BAD HAPPENS TO ME?

My intention was to end this chapter here, but a meeting with a woman who attended one of my motivational seminars changed my mind. She told me that she would be sure to come to the next one as well. She said that the technique of anchoring (it's described in the chapter about motivation) helped her greatly, and it also helped her when we were getting rid of fears and limiting beliefs. But she still had some fears remaining that had been consuming her since she could remember.

Her biggest fear was that something would happen to her (injury or death) or to her children. She was afraid for her life, because she did not know how she would manage in life by herself. To the question of where this fear of hers originated, she answered that nothing in her life had happened of which she should be afraid. However, I wanted to get to the point of identifying the important emotional event in her life.

I then asked her which question she asks herself most often and when she is afraid. She replied, "Constantly I ask myself, what if something bad happens to me?" When I asked her which words from her parents she remembered the most, she told me, "Be careful of something bad happening to you!"

I watched her facial expression and hand gestures while she was saying this. I suggested that she repeat the words of her parents, and simultaneously use other hand gestures. Before, she had very carefully put her hands together as if praying in a triangle - that was her mother's gesture when she warned her against "bad" things. Then, she said the sentence as if she were telling somebody, "F...off!" She laughed loudly. At that moment, because of the new funny gestures, she started to connect other images in her head. In this way, the woman was capable in every moment of altering her feelings. Her new primary question is, "What marvelous things can I still experience?" You probably noticed that she was just continuing the patterns of her parents, and passed them on to her own children.

Questions like that are also common to salesmen, businessmen, managers, and many others. Some have bigger fears and limiting beliefs than others. But all of them could live better lives if they used the techniques that I describe in this book. I have decided to tape the techniques for overcoming various fears and limiting beliefs, which I have described in the passage about the virus of success, so that people can easily help themselves. In this way, help will be more efficient.

3. YOUR THOUGHTS (WHAT YOU FOCUS ON) AND YOUR BELIEFS ABOUT CERTAIN THINGS

Let me ask you some more questions: What has to happen for you to become successful? How can you start to be aware of your greatest potential? When will you begin to keep track of a great number of actions? What will motivate you to improve and change your beliefs about what you are capable of?

Each level of progress in the areas described can increase your success. Most progress happens when you change your limiting beliefs about your capabilities. The majority of us still use only 10% of our potential. Can you imagine what would happen to the quality of your life in all the areas if you used only an additional 10% of your capabilities?

Let us say, for example, that, based on your previous experiences, you are aware that you are not the best at a certain task. Perhaps in being aware that you do not have the highest abilities in a certain field, you will realize that you do not give as much effort to improving as you should. Maybe you do very little or even nothing to improve. Because you will not take all the steps you should, you will get the results you deserve. If, when you notice poor results, you start to nurse the belief that in that area you simply are not good enough, you will soon slide down into THE MAGICAL ABYSS OF FAILURE.

> "What we focus on expands."
> - Arnold Patent

If you focus your attention to the areas in which you are good or even naturally talented, your self-confidence will grow. You will get excited over what you are capable of doing. As soon as you see bigger possibilities for success, you try even harder and get even better results. The results that you achieve then deepen your belief in what are you capable of. That MAGICAL CIRCLE OF SUCCESS must be established in your life if you want to achieve fantastic results, and you have to keep to the path you designed yourself. The choice is yours. Change your system of limiting beliefs, and you will change your destiny. We can assure you of that.

MARTA AND LIMITING BELIEFS

Marta's dream was to own a company. Because of a series of fears and limiting beliefs, she did not accomplish this until the seminar on motivation. Just a week after the seminar, in which we exercised the process of exchanging limiting beliefs and fears, she established her own company and made her long-cherished dream become reality. How many and which dreams could you realize if you got rid of limiting beliefs and fears?

THE POWER OF POSITIVE BELIEFS

Here is another example of what can happen if you change limiting beliefs. Years ago, all runners, as well as the general public and sports professionals, were of the belief that a human being is not capable of running one mile in less than four minutes. For 20 years, the record was 4 minutes and 1.4 seconds. Everybody believed that the record could not be surpassed. The only one who did not believe that was a medical student, Roger Bannister, who practiced running mentally as well as physically. He imagined for himself very vividly how he could run one mile in less than four minutes. On the 6th of May, 1954, he surprised the world public when he ran one mile in a time of 3 minutes and 59.4 seconds.

> "In the beginning, people don't want to believe that it is possible to realize something unusual; then, slowly, they start to hope that it might happen, and then they do it, and they wonder afterwards.
> - Frances Hodgson Burnett

Right after Roger Bannister gave up limiting beliefs, other runners realized that it was possible to run the mile under four minutes. Just two months after that historical run, Bannister's own record was broken. In the two years after his venture, more than one hundred runners ran the mile in less than four minutes. When Roger overcame the old belief and all the fears, he encouraged others to overcome the mental obstacle about the mile distance as well.

Dr. Victor Frankl spent several years in a concentration camp and survived, despite all the horrible things that were happening there. He lived by the belief that only 10% of what happens to us in our life is important and the other 90% depends on what significance we give to it. Later, I will introduce a process which we perform at the motivational seminar and which has changed many lives.

FEAR AND LIMITING BELIEFS - EXCUSES FOR INACTIVITY

Did you ever have dreams, goals or wishes which you really wanted to realize? Have you forgotten most of those dreams already? Did you have plans and ideas, which somehow became drowned in oblivion?

If that is the case, may I help you? I will reveal the secret of why that happened to you. Because of fears and limiting beliefs, you lost faith in what you once wanted so badly. In a few moments, you are going to be able to set out once more on the path of your previous wishes and goals.

> "One can never consent to creep when one feels the impulse to soar."
> - Helen Keller

Five years ago, when I found myself at a turning point in my life, and I wanted to make the most of my life, I found within myself many reasons that were the obstacles to my starting my own company. Only later did I discover that these were just excuses - the consequences of fear and limiting beliefs that prevented me from living life as I do now.

MY LIMITING BELIEFS:

- I am too young to start my own company.
- I do not have any experience in running a business.
- I do not have any money to start a business.
- I am too highly educated to sell life insurance policies.

- People will not trust me because I used to work as a criminologist.
- I do not know enough people.
- I do not have the knowledge for the job.
- What if I don't succeed?

These were the beliefs that I nurtured in my head. When I managed to get rid of them, I achieved in five years incredible progress in personal and professional areas.

Let us examine further the other limiting beliefs that can cause fear and stand in the way to success, and which produce excuses for not actively pursuing our goals.

ENCHANTED CIRCLE OF FAILURE

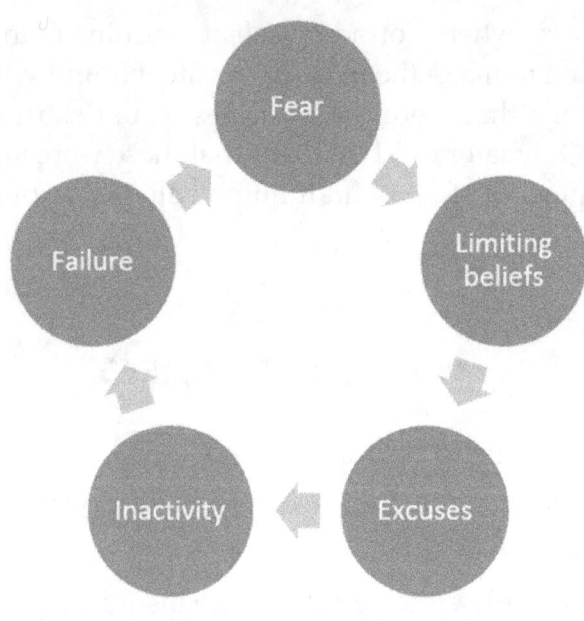

Let us see how the enchanted circle of failure works.

Because of various fears and limiting beliefs, we start using excuses with which we excuse our deeds or thoughts. So we begin to accumulate rational reasons why we don't do something, or why we have done something. We do not call these things excuses but, instead, convince ourselves with sentences like this, "I cannot; it won't work; I don't know how; not now because…" Then, because we start to believe these excuses, we become inactive. Inactivity in any field leads to failure. The more failures we go through, the more we get frightened and the more limiting beliefs we acquire for other areas of our lives. Moreover, when we keep repeating various excuses, we actually start to believe in them. In order to achieve success and progress in our lives, we first have to cut the thick cord linking us to our fears and excuses. After we do that, we start to take other actions and we get different results.

In my work, I have met many people who want to become salespeople. They always offer me logical explanations of why they cannot start to sell: they do not have time; this is not for them; the time is not right yet; they are busy with other things. It is true that each person is not right for every job, and it is true that in sales, you have to face rejection. That is the hardest part of such work. Only those salespersons who can overcome the fear of rejection can forge an excellent career.

I concluded that there are three things either that make people successful or that cause them to lie down on the rocks of defeat:

1. Fears and limiting beliefs
2. Decisions
3. Actions and deeds

Successful people could overcome certain fears and limiting beliefs. They made decisions that were followed by action.

Here are some limiting beliefs of people that I have encountered during seminars:

- I am too old.
- I am a woman.
- I do not know how to sell.
- I cannot make social contact with people.
- I cannot afford that.
- I am too fat.
- I am not attractive.
- I have not finished university.
- I am not educated enough.
- I am too lazy.
- Money spoils people.
- People do not like me.
- My husband/wife does not love me.
- I am afraid of what others will say.
- I am afraid of being without a job.

7 STEPS TO CONTROL NEGATIVE BELIEFS

This approach can be used whenever you would like to get rid of limiting beliefs in any area of your life and also if you would like to get rid of certain bad habits relating to career, family, relationships, health, nutrition, smoking, or overeating.

1st STEP: IDENTIFY

Think of which beliefs stop you on the way to success, happiness and contentment. Be honest with yourself because only in that way can you progress in your life.

2nd STEP: WRITE IT DOWN

Write down five of the biggest fears and limiting beliefs that have been haunting you for a long time and are obstacles on your way to success.

EXERCISE 26

My limiting beliefs and fears:

1._____
2._____
3._____
4._____
5._____

3rd STEP: EVOKE THE PAIN

In the third step, you will associate, as much as possible, physical pain with your old, limiting beliefs. The more you are sure that you cannot change, the more pain you will feel. Look upon your limiting beliefs and experience the pain you will feel five, ten, fifteen, and twenty years from now - if you do not change course. Meanwhile, ask yourself questions that will create pain. Do not worry if you cry or get upset. That is actually the aim - for you to say, "That's enough! I've had enough; never again!"

Questions to cause pain:

- What will your refusal to change mean to the financial side of your life?
- What will it mean for your relationships?
- What are you going to miss in your life?
- What have you already missed because of living with limiting beliefs and fears?
- What could you achieve if you did not have them?
- Who will leave you if you are not going to change?
- What are you going to say to your children? How will you have to lie to them?
- Who have you already disappointed because you insist on your fears and limiting beliefs?
- How long are you going to live like this?
- Who are you not going to meet?
- Are you planning to live the next five, ten, fifteen, twenty years with the same fears and limiting beliefs?

4th STEP: DEFLATE THE BELIEFS

The fourth step is both amusing and effective. Read your limiting beliefs in funny voices (like in an old movie) and even make faces at the same time. Make sure no one sees! This is an effective way of mentally transforming fears and limiting beliefs, because you do not take them seriously afterward. Before you move on to the next step, make sure that you do the third one because it may be very important.

5th STEP: WRITE DOWN NEW BELIEFS

Now, write down your negative beliefs in a positive way. Written like this, they will give you strength and energy for big achievements. Write something that can give you self-confidence. Beware — you must have no doubts about your new belief! You have to be 100% sure of it because you probably knew about it already, but you never dared say it aloud.

OLD BELIEF	NEW BELIEF
I'm too old	The fifties are going to be the most productive years of my life. I have the experience of five people half my age.

EXERCISE 27

MY OLD BELIEFS	MY NEW BELIEFS
1._____	1._____
2._____	2._____
3._____	3._____
4._____	4._____
5._____	5._____

6th STEP: DESTROY YOUR OLD BELIEFS

Crossing out or writing down negative thoughts on a special piece of paper that you tear into many pieces and throw away can destroy old beliefs.

7th STEP: KEEP REPEATING YOUR NEW BELIEFS

Repeat your new positive beliefs with heavy emotional emphasis. Simultaneously, count the logical reasons why you are sure that these beliefs are the right ones.

WHAT WOULD YOU SAY ABOUT THESE PEOPLE IF YOU HADN'T HEARD ABOUT THEIR SUCCESSES?

Ronald Reagan was 69 years old when he first ran for the presidency. Many were of the belief that he was too old, but despite that he ran the country successfully and was also re-elected. Colonel Sanders started his chain KFC (Kentucky Fried Chicken) after his retirement.

George Burns received an Oscar when he was 80 years old.

Neither Henry Ford nor Abraham Lincoln had achieved much success before their forties. On the other hand, Mozart wrote his first composition at the age of eight.

> *"One's own self conquered is better than conquering all other people."*
> — Dhammapada

Not all these people cared much what others thought, and they didn't concern themselves with whether they were capable of doing it or not. They simply believed in their vision and followed their goals until they achieved them.

ARE YOU EMOTIONALLY TOO ATTACHED?

Has it ever happened to you that you could not forget one person or event that made a big impression on you? Once I was talking to a young woman who confessed that she fell into depressions. The depression started after she was separated from her brother.

I tried to comfort her by saying, "With your brother, you were walking the same path for nine years. Each path separates somewhere into two or newer ones. Some separate earlier, some later." Definitely, their path had separated too soon.

I asked her if she could imagine her separation as two different paths leading to the same destination. The goal was happiness, contentment and love. For now, she and her brother are just walking on their own paths of experience, which one day, after they reach their destinations, will converge. On each path, obstacles will appear.

She has two choices: either to go around them or to jump over them, or she can sit down and start to complain how life is cruel to put such obstacles in her way. She can weep, cry, and even go back the same way. But in so doing, she will never meet her brother waiting for her to share all the secrets he has learned. She will never be able to give him her love if she does not reach the destination – their destination.

She decided to fight all the obstacles that come her way. She chose this route so that she can one day transfer all her experiences to others she loves and cares about; she has to walk her part of the path.

Similarly, many times in your life you will walk in a path which you cannot find your way through at first. When you look around, you will see that there was also some pleasant scenery along on the way, and new things you had to learn.

GET RID OF UNNECESSARY WORRY AND FEAR AND EMBRACE SUCCESS

When I studied success and successful people, I concluded: everybody who succeeded in life and achieved big things had something in common. Nobody - not one - worried too much about what could happen on the way to success!

After I realized that fear, worry and limiting beliefs are what eats up the human soul, I committed myself to invest all my energy to master these emotional conditions.

One of my passions is also teaching people to throw fear out of their personal or professional lives by getting it out of their heads. They ask me how it is possible that after only one motivational seminar they can change so much, or make such progress in their personal and professional lives. My answer stays the same: "Because you got rid of unnecessary worries, doubts and limiting beliefs."

> **"Worry achieves nothing; it just wastes time."**
> - John M. Templeton

Unnecessary worries steal our time and energy. They often hide like shadows of our life in some hidden corner of doubt or uncertainty. They can interrupt us when we are asleep, destroy our capabilities for making decisions and steal the happiness and contentment that we could have experienced. When we are worried, we do not plan our activities, we do not pursue the way to our goals. When we become obsessed with a certain problem and worry, we avoid making decisions and initiating activities.

When I analyze why I worry, I conclude that my worries are caused by four kinds of anxiety.

Usually I worry because of:

1. Decisions I have to make.
2. Activities which I should participate in but which I am avoiding.
3. Events that I can affect.
4. Events, which I cannot affect.

> **"Unnecessary worries steal our time and energy. They are often hidden like shadows of our life in some hidden corner of doubt and uncertainty."**
> - Smiljan Mori

Studies of the anxiety show how much unnecessary time we spend on insignificant worries and fears:

- 40% of the things we worry about never happen.
- 30% of worries appear because of things that happened in the past, and about which we can now do nothing.
- 12% of worries are hidden in thoughts about other people and things that do not concern us at all.
- 10% of worries cause diseases, real or imagined.
- 8% are worries that do affect us and on which we should focus.

As we can see, 82% of all worries are unnecessary and only absorb time and energy; almost 80% of our time, we dedicate to resolve those worries. Only 20% of our time is dedicated to the worries which affect us and which we can influence. We have to be careful not to dedicate 80% of our time to problems and only 20% of our time to the solutions. This ratio should be reversed.

Many books deal solely with how to overcome worries and problems, but I will give you only one piece of advice that helped me a lot.

THREE KINDS OF THINGS ABOUT WHICH WE SHOULD NOT EVER WORRY

First: We should not worry about things which we cannot change and on which we cannot have an influence.

If we cannot change them, then a melancholy mood and worry are equally ineffective. These are things that have happened already.

Secondly: We should not worry about things that have not happened yet.

When they happen, we will see if we can solve them or not. We worry unnecessarily about eventual personal or professional problems. Until something actually happens, it does not make sense to worry about it.

Thirdly: We should not worry about things that we can change.

If we can affect things and change them, we have to start taking measures for their solution. We should not waste our time on unfruitful moaning. We should never worry about things we can still affect or change. We just have to take action!

STOP WORRYING AND START LIVING

Although my work is to teach people how to use their thinking capacities to achieve happiness, success, wealth and contentment, I often tell them that they should use their heads less and their hands and legs more. In other words, overcome the fear and worry with a number of actions that will lead you toward your goal.

When you become worried, you focus on the future instead of the present. By worrying, you are wasting your precious time, like throwing away tomorrow's opportunity with a preoccupation with problems from the past.

> "Keep yourself busy with where you are going and not where you have been."
> - John M. Templeton

THIS IS NOT THAT

A frequent mistake we all make is that we always compare THIS and THAT. However, THIS isn't THAT and THAT isn't THIS. If THIS were THAT and if THAT was THIS, then everything would be the SAME. But it is not that way. We are comparing the past with the future too much, and we build our future based on the past. That does not mean that you should not learn from the mistakes you made in the past. I am just trying to suggest to you that you should not build your future on the negative basis of the past.

IF YOU DON'T LIKE THE TENANT, THROW HIM OUT

In my work with people who suffer because of various fears, phobias or limiting beliefs, I realized that when they are in a certain condition, they always focus on the same images. These are the pictures they have taped when they were in a very negative emotional condition and which haunt them all their lives.

For example: you have two flats that you rent to two different tenants. The first is a GOOD tenant: he pays regularly; he is kind and pleasant; he often cheers you up and because of that, you are happy and contented. The other is BAD: he does not pay the rent on time, and he makes you depressed, angry, sad and moody. What would you do if you had a BAD tenant in your flat? You would certainly evict him.

Why don't you throw out of your head the pictures which constantly irritate you, put you in a bad mood and cause anger, fear and depression? Let me ask you again: "Would you go to the theatre to watch a movie again if you didn't even like it the first time?" Of course, you would not go back a second time... Why, then, do you replay in your head tapes you don't like?

For more than ten years, I have known people who have suffered because of their phobias and fears. Some tried to commit suicide; some were constantly depressed, sad or nervous. Then, there are the top athletes who have experienced major setbacks in their careers, salesmen who were afraid of being rejected, successful businessmen and individuals who were afraid of losing their jobs. All of them were nervous. I have noticed in everybody a common pattern: they kept focusing on the same picture - a picture that brought about in them certain negative emotions and conditions.

TECHNIQUES TO OVERCOME FEARS AND PHOBIAS

Not long ago, I was working with a woman who suffered from severe depression. When I asked her to close her eyes, go into a depressed mood and tell me what picture she saw, she told me that she saw a picture of her deceased mother. With the technique of double dissociation, (an NLP technique which I will describe later) I helped her in 15 minutes to change her feelings towards that picture and removed a key obstacle from her path to a better life.

1. Before you start performing the techniques to get rid of phobias, or if you would like to get rid of something that bothers you, you have to create a strong kinesthetic anchor (touch – see the chapter on motivation). Just imagine that you are sitting in the theatre and in front of your eyes unrolls a movie, which causes in you negative feelings and emotional reactions.

2. After you get accustomed to this, imagine that you leave your body and, in your mind, go to the balcony where from a distance, in a safe shelter, you watch what is unfolding on the screen.

3. Then, imagine that the upsetting movie has begun. Describe precisely what picture you see (colored, black and white, still or moving). In this moment, you are watching the event without being emotionally involved. Actually, you are watching yourself from the balcony, as if you are watching a screen where the movie with negative events is playing. You can participate in the action on the screen, or you can just watch the movie if it bothers you. You have to pay attention to your reactions. If you notice that you are getting afraid again, come back to the here and now. The best would be

to clench your hand into a fist and keep it that way all the time. This way, you will feel that reality is here with you and not on the screen. You will realize that the problem lies within. With all your emotional and physical involvement, imagine a situation that bothers you. Imagine this situation so that you feel as if what has happened to you in the past is happening now.

4. Take the negative picture on the screen, and scramble it so that it will be funny to you. Attach big donkey ears or a clown nose on the person who disturbs you in the movie; distort the voice and words that bother you. The next time you think of the situation that used to be so bothersome, you will have to smile, because you are now going to see a different, funny picture.

5. Now, return to your body and go to the screen, where you tell the younger you that you are from the future, and that he does not need to be afraid of these pictures because they are just a movie. Sit back in the chair and invite your younger self back into your body.

6. Test the completed work. When you finish the procedure, divert your attention for a moment with some other question; then, think again about the event that bothered you. If you smile, it means that you have performed the procedure correctly.

Now you know how to overcome fears and limiting beliefs. It is time to look at:

SECRET #4:

THE HEART OF MOTIVATION

HEALTH

Good-bye health; forgive me but I haven't got time for you. Come back, try again, please wait; I don't have time now. I would like to exercise, but I haven't got time. I cannot help myself. I eat whatever I get; in that way, I save time. I cannot think. I cannot read. I'm trapped. I don't have time. I would like to live, but I don't have time. When I'm dead, you'll be gone. And I'm going to ask myself, "Why did I never have TIME?"

Anonymous

IN THIS CHAPTER, YOU WILL FIND OUT:

9 pieces of advice which could be given to you by your physician, which may come too late.

ଔ

What are the emotional causes of overeating.

ଔ

How to get rid of 15 pounds in only five weeks with the help of your thoughts.

ଔ

How to control your weight with the help of your thoughts.

ଔ

Why water is so important for general health.

ଔ

How to get rid of surplus weight forever.

ଔ

12 motivational steps towards life without cigarettes.

ଔ

How to increase dramatically the level of your energy.

HEALTH

THE STORY OF YOUR LIFE AND MINE

Five years have passed since you set yourself the task of buying a new car. Now, your dreams are realized. You are standing in front of a dealership and holding the keys to your new car. You sit proudly behind the wheel and turn the key. The indicator for gas reminds you that you have to stop at the nearest gas station. The salesman reminds you that you have gas for only ten miles.

The town you live in is about 70 miles away from the dealership. You certainly will not make it to your goal with the gas you have. But you do not care, and you let yourself enjoy the ride in your new car (you do not care much about your health). You simply forget about the fuel. Suddenly, the car starts to jump (you have caught a slight cold). What is that, you ask yourself? O my God, I forgot to put gas in the tank (now you get seriously sick). How will I reach home (you become concerned about your health)? What a pity that I did not think about that before and fill up on gas (from this day forwards now on I will really take care of my health). I will buy some as soon as I reach the gas station (from now on I will really pay attention to what I eat).

> "The human body is the best picture of the human soul."
> - Ludwig Wittgenstein

You stand by the road waving to drivers and asking them for help (you visit an emergency doctor). Luckily, somebody pulls over and lends you some spare gas (you are waiting in the hospital). You are glad that you have enough gas to reach the gas station (thank God; it is not serious). With this gas, you barely get yourself to the gas station, and you are relieved (you forget what you just promised). You step out of the car and pour in the gas fast because you are in a hurry to get home (you are pursuing your everyday goals, but you forgot the important things). Relieved, you turn the key and drive toward your home (your goal in life). After a few miles, the car stops again (again something is wrong with your health). You stand by the road again waving to those who pass by, and you hope that somebody will have pity on you (you are in the waiting room again, but now it is worse). You tell yourself, "Why now, I'm in a hurry (Oh, dear; I don't have time to be sick because I have to work). Finally, somebody shows some compassion and tells you that you made a mistake and added the wrong fuel (now you are seriously ill). You just cannot believe that you will not be home on time.

With a car like that, you cannot go on. You leave the car there and call somebody to tow your car for service (the doctor finds that the situation is critical; you have to stop eating greasy food, meat and salt and to give up smoking, alcohol and also avoid stressful situations, otherwise you are doomed). Finally, you pull yourself together and take the advice. What comes next you (probably) know already. How could I write a story like that you ask yourself? Because I lived this story, at the age of 28.

I DON'T HAVE TIME TO EXERCISE BECAUSE I HAVE TO WORK

I used that excuse for so long that one day I was barely able to drag myself upstairs into my office on the second floor. My heart was thumping; I felt pressure in my head; my legs were weak, and I had no will or energy. The only way I knew to get energy was to drink sweet, strong coffee. Then I said to myself, "I've got it! How will all this money help me, if I cannot even breathe? By the age of 50, I'll be worm's meat." That was the greatest pain that I had ever experienced. Because of it, I vowed to do anything for increased well-being and a healthy lifestyle. Since then, nearly two years have passed, and the level of my energy today is obvious. At that time, I was usually completely worn out by four o'clock in the afternoon. In a few months, I changed my nutrition; in 10 months, I lost about 30 pounds (a little bit too much for such a short time, but I did not know enough about nutrition at that time). Nevertheless, despite the correct nutritional habits and working out, I regained, in 8 months, about 24 pounds. Now, however, the weight is better distributed throughout my body. I feel better;

I have more energy so that I am able to work for 16 hours daily. Of course, I go to the fitness center for two hours in that 16-hour day. Despite that, I run two companies and, with more commitment and less time, I can always manage to take care of my body and, most important of all, to provide my body with the right fuel.

> "An important scientific innovation rarely makes its way by gradually winning over and converting its opponents. What does happen is that its opponents gradually die, and that the growing generation is familiarized with the ideas from the beginning."
> - Max Planck

WE ARE WHAT WE EAT

I do not want to go into detail about healthy nutrition and get into a discussion about proper food, because there is plenty of professional literature already written about it. I believe you know a lot about it already. I will focus instead on emotional reasons that make many people fight with weight problems almost all their lives. I will describe only what worked for many others and me. The decision is up to you what you are going to do about it. I will also share with you how some of the participants in my motivational seminar "miraculously" lost weight - 22 pounds in two months - and improved their self-image. A warning: before you start with any diet, consult your physician.

HEALTH

9 ADVICE THAT MAY BE GIVEN BY YOUR PHYSICIAN, WHICH MAY COME TOO LATE

1. THE POWER OF BREATHING

Correct breathing demands from us the uses of the membrane that divides the chest cavity from the stomach. In correct breathing, the membrane shrinks and pushes the stomach forward, which allows the lungs to expand and fill with air. To have the greatest possible use from the approximately 11.500 liters of air we daily inhale, we should learn to breathe in from the bottom and all the way up. If you perform this exercise at least three times daily, your level of energy will increase by 20%.

The exercise for efficient breathing is:

3 times daily, breathe 10 times in, deeply, according to the following procedure:

- first exhale
- breathe in 4 seconds
- hold for 16 seconds
- exhale for 8 seconds

If inhalation lasts 4 seconds, you have to hold your breath for 16 seconds (multiply inhalation time by 4) and then exhale for 8 seconds (multiply inhalation time by 2). This kind of breathing will fill you with energy immediately; you will become more motivated and productive.

2. BEFORE NOON, EAT ONLY FRUITS AND VEGETABLES

In the past, I could not agree with this idea because every morning, I used to eat at least four pieces of bread with different spreads, drink 3 dl of multivitamin juice and top all of that off with yogurt. Before ten, I was hungry again and under stress. When I tried fruits and vegetables, I immediately had more energy for work; besides that, I became more focused and creative. Eat fruit only on an empty stomach. For at least two hours after that, do not eat anything. Do not eat fruit with any other food.

3. THE RIGHT WAY TO COMBINE FOOD

The correct combination of food that was given to us by Mother Nature demands minimal effort from our digestive system. We spend much more energy to digest meat than to digest fruit, vegetables or starches. After I started to combine food in the proper way, tiredness after lunch disappeared miraculously. Now, after my lunch, which is, by the way, bigger than in the past, I can work with the same level of energy as prior to lunch. Before I started with this regime, I had to rest for about an hour and a half after lunch. Maybe you disagree with me about this right now. Even I disagreed, at first, because I was brought up with other beliefs that still influenced my eating habits. I am disappointed that they did not teach us proper nutrition at school. Try it for yourself and you will be surprised with the results!

> "If your stomach could talk, what would it tell you after a big meal? Would it thank you, or would it be angry with you?"
>
> Smiljan Mori

This diagram shows which sort of food we should not combine..

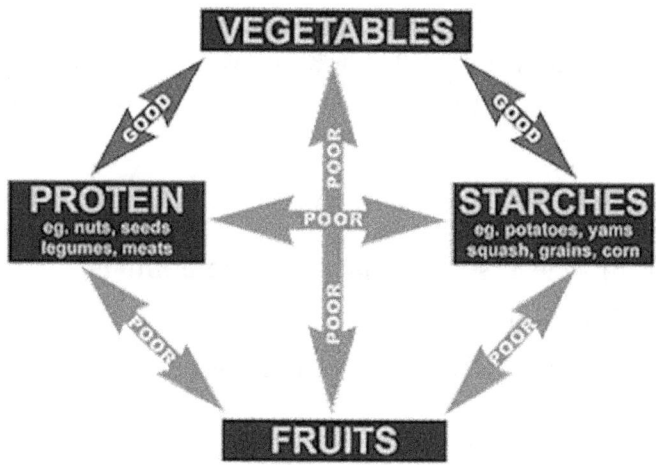

4. DRINK ENOUGH WATER DURING THE DAY

It may sound incredible, but water is probably the best catalyst to losing and maintaining body weight. Water, in a natural way, decreases the appetite and helps the body to metabolize fats. Every day, we should drink at least three liters of water (not beer, juice, soda pops or colas…). Next time you are hungry or without energy, perform the breathing exercise and drink a glass of water - immediately you will feel better. Never, however, drink water while eating, because it impedes digestion. Do not drink it after a meal either. Drink it at least 15 minutes before the meal.

5. DRAMATICALLY REDUCE THE MEAT AND DAIRY PRODUCTS CONSUMED

The negative consequences of meat consumption (for us and for the planet) were studied by John Robbins in the book Diet for a New America.

Robbins founded Earthsave to demonstrate the following facts:

- In the USA, 40% of cancers are connected to nutrition.
- The risk of breast cancer in women who eat meat every day is, in comparison with those who eat it once a week, 3.8% higher.

If you really are a meat eater, try to follow this advice:

1. Buy from a clean source (naturally fed animals).
2. Eat meat only once a day.
3. Consume meat in the right combinations.

When it comes to milk and dairy, I can only point out: COWS DON'T DRINK COW'S MILK - WHY SHOULD YOU? You can get calcium elsewhere.

6. SAY NO TO COFFEE, NICOTINE, ALCOHOL AND SUGAR

I know that it is hard to give them up, but if you are honest with yourself, you will have to admit that we are more emotionally than physically addicted to them.

7. THE MORE YOU READ, THE MORE YOU WILL KNOW

With every new book I read about nutrition, I become aware of how little I still know about it. I will admit, I used to know almost nothing. Actually, I knew only what my parents taught me (that we have to eat), and what they were taught about nutrition by their parents and so on. Different questions occur to me as I watch more and more people having problems with obesity. I am talking about this difficult topic because I care about your life - perhaps you still do not. When you delve more into books about healthy nutrition, you might be confused because some of these are contradictory. The best you can do is to test them in practice or to attend one of our seminars. Together with the experts, we will help you to understand how to eliminate the different unhealthy eating habits you have been used to.

> "The biggest obstacle to change is a wrong pattern of thinking".
> - Anonymous

8. THE POWER OF AEROBIC EXERCISE

For greater well-being, higher efficiency and less stress, I suggest you work up a sweat at least three times a week. You know - bicycle, run or swim. Do not think that because of that, you will not have enough time for work; on the contrary, in a shorter period, you will be able to produce much more.

9. FIND YOURSELF A PERSONAL COACH

Nobody can do everything themselves. Do not be embarrassed to admit that you are not sufficiently competent in certain areas. Because we all need help, it is a good idea to find yourself a personal coach who will help you with advice and encourage you in areas where you could accomplish more. Although I perform personal counseling to help people achieve better results than the ones they could achieve by themselves, I have a personal coach for physical exercise. Therefore, I suggest you consult first with experts before you start working out and changing your eating habits. You will save valuable time and money.

> "Let us take care of our bodies because our bodies take care of our health."
> Smiljan Mori

IF YOU ARE SLIM, THAT DOESN'T NECESSARILY MEAN THAT YOU ARE HEALTHY

Many people are of the belief that they are healthy if they do not have extra weight to carry around. Some believe that if they are vegetarian, they live a healthy lifestyle. They eat ice cream and candies; they smoke and drink coffee. Health and physical condition are not considered. Health means having a perpetual source of energy.

THE DEPARTMENT OF OVEREATING

CHANGE THE WAY YOU EAT AND YOU WILL NEVER NEED A DIET AGAIN

If you would like to lose surplus weight and maintain that perfect weight, you will have to change your eating habits. Never again say the words "diet" and "losing weight" because these words mean pain for your brain. Which sounds better: if I say that you will have to lose weight, or if I say that you must just change your eating habits a bit? Which would you rather do?

When I started to work with a group of five who decided to lose weight for the last time, sorry, I mean, change their eating habits, we talked in the first hour about the psychic pain that we feel when we have to lose weight. We feel pain because our brain is connected to giving up the food with which we are addicted. We have to face our limiting beliefs about nutrition.

These go something like this:

We know that we will have to exercise a bit more, which is not very appealing in the beginning. We connect all of that with the thought that the new diet regime will not last forever, but only until we lose a few pounds. So, in the very beginning, our brains are programmed that this will not last forever. As soon we achieve our goal, we fall back into our old eating habits. We start saying to ourselves, "Only this piece, it cannot hurt me; it doesn't contain very many calories" or" just today, but after the new year no more." Do you recognize this pattern? If we say to ourselves that we are "going on a diet", it also automatically means that at some point we are "going off the diet" as well.

Before we go into a deeper analysis of overeating, read the following questions, which were also answered by participants in therapy sessions that helped them to lose weight forever.

It will be very useful if you answer these questions for yourself as well:

1. Why have you decided to lose weight?
2. With what do you connect losing weight? Does this represent pain or pleasure for you?
3. If it represents pain, answer why.
4. What are you afraid of if you stay the way you are?
5. What are your beliefs about food, nutrition, losing weight? What do others tell you about nutrition and losing weight, which has affected you a great deal?
6. What is your favorite food? What food couldn't you give up at all?
7. What food do you only have to think about to see or smell, to make your mouth water?
8. What food disgusts you, so that you cannot see it, and definitely cannot eat it?
9. In your past, have you ever given up something but been overcome by temptation again?
10. Until now, what has hurt you the most that you would not like to happen again?
11. What negative experiences have you gone through because of your obesity?

> "A healthy spirit helps you to a healthy body, and vice versa."
> - John M. Templeton

12. What will happen to you if you do not start living in a healthier way?
13. Of all the things you are most afraid of in your life, which is connected with your bad habits?

14. Why would you like to be healthy, good-looking and in peak condition?
15. What do you say to yourself when you catch yourself falling into unhealthy eating habits?
16. Who or what is to blame for the way you are today and your dissatisfaction with yourself?
17. How much do you weigh right now?
18. How much would you like to weigh? When would you like to achieve your ideal weight?
19. How do you see yourself 5, 10, and 15 years from now?
20. With what did you always comfort yourself?
21. What were your excuses when you wanted to lose weight or start to work out?
22. What comes to mind when I say to you, "Tomorrow you will start losing weight".
23. Find an unflattering picture of yourself that shows how overweight you are. Show someone this picture and explain that you no longer want to look like that.
24. Find a picture from when you still had a fabulous figure. If you do not have this kind of picture, find one of somebody else who has the figure you would like to have.

WHY DO WE OVEREAT, DRINK ALCOHOL AND SMOKE?

Many people focus only on the body while losing weight. When we are talking about the body and losing weight, we have to know that in the word body, we must combine not only the body (physically) but also the emotions and the psychological state.

I believe that people overeat because of emotions. Emotions are also to blame for addiction to certain foods, cigarettes, alcohol, and candy. Emotions make it so that we cannot give up addictions that easily. When I ask participants in the seminar or my clients in personal consultation, why they started overeating, drinking coffee, alcohol or using drugs, and why they are not able to stop, I get varied and contradictory answers. However, I have concluded that it is all in the mind. You can have ten different diets, but none of them will help you if you do not change some things in your mind.

Mrs. Bernarda, who seemed fat and jolly, told me that she had tried to lose weight many times, but she always failed. There were always friends to tell her that she should stay as she was. So, she started to connect her cheerful attitude with her obesity. Her brain told her, "If you stay fat (and jolly), people will always like you."

It was different with Andreja, who lost about 30 pounds in only 4 weeks after our meetings (which occurred once a week for 1.5 hours). Yes, you have read correctly. Since then, nearly nine months have passed, and Andreja now weighs about 45 pounds less than when we first met. She started to overeat because she felt inferior at school. She also blamed her parents because, in her childhood, she could not leave the table until she had finished the meal.

Andreja had other causes for overeating. In her childhood, her family had suffered for lack of food, so now because of the fear of being hungry again, she always ate too much.

As you can see, our participants were driven to overeat by different emotional events and distinct limiting beliefs. What emotional causes lead you to overeat or to indulge in any other bad habit? If you are satisfied with your health and looks, then this does not apply to you. However, you are able to transfer these words and questions to other areas that you would like to change.

Just yesterday, I asked two people why they started to smoke. The first one told me that it had seemed so fabulous. Everybody in his gang was smoking, and it was a blast. The other person told me that she started to smoke out of stress, anger and sleepless nights. Each person has his or her own unique excuses and reasons for starting to smoke.

QUESTIONNAIRE ON THE "EMOTIONAL CAUSES" OF OVEREATING

Which of the following emotional causes applies to you? Your emotions before overeating, in between, and after are very important to discovering strategies that will work effectively for you.

Do you eat when you feel lonely?

Do you eat when you feel angry?

Do you eat when you feel dissatisfied?

Do you eat when you are under pressure?

Do you eat when you are happy?

Do you eat when you are nervous, anxious?

Do you eat when you are afraid of something?

Do you eat when you are socializing?

How do you feel after overeating?

What do you say to yourself after you have eaten what you should not?

When you find out which emotions are causing your overeating, you must identify the triggering emotional condition and then replace your old reaction with something else that won't hurt you. For example, breathe deeply, go for a stroll, sing or drink a glass of water.

THE DEPARTMENT OF MENTAL DIET

USE THE TECHNIQUE OF PAIN - PLEASURE

Now, after you've truthfully answered all these questions, what lies ahead of you will be your "RECIPE, I.E. STRATEGY AGAINST OVEREATING"

What do you have to do if you want to spoil the taste of the cake, which we baked in the chapter about motivation? You just add some more ingredients. Likewise, with your recipe against overeating: you have to change limiting beliefs, thoughts and words. Those things we have talked about already.

> "Let us avoid the pleasures which bring us pain afterward and let us yearn for pains that will bring us more happiness and satisfaction."
> - Michel De Montaigne

What would happen to your cake if you baked it at too high a temperature? It will burn. Would you eat it anyhow? Probably, you would not. Even so, you must eat it if you want to change your eating habits by associating your present condition and limiting beliefs with enormous psychic pain.

HEALTH

You have to ask yourself what would happen to you in 5, 10, 15 years from now if you stick with today's habits. Use the same procedure as in the chapter about limiting beliefs.

THINK HEALTHY; EAT WITH THE HEAD, OR THE TECHNIQUE OF THOUGHTFUL PLEASURE

The technique I describe in this chapter, is one you are already using subconsciously, only you are using it now against yourself; now, you will consciously use it in your favor.

Check how you answered question #7 in the Department of Overeating. If you have not done that yet, you have to go back and answer the questions, unless you are already satisfied with yourself. But you should still check if you have answered all the other questions in this book. It cannot hurt you, really!

Now, close your eyes and start to picture yourself eating your favorite food (ice cream, pizza, hamburger, etc.). Enjoy it and taste it because these are your very last bites. Did your mouth start to water? Do you have the feeling that you will have to go straight to the fridge? Are you hungry? Now, open your eyes and recall your most hated food. Close your eyes, and start to picture that you have this disgusting food in your mouth... you are biting it, swallowing...tasting this repugnant stuff.

> *"Nature has placed mankind under the governance of two sovereign masters, pain and pleasure...they govern us in all we do, in all we say, in all we think: every effort we can make to throw off our subjection, will serve but to demonstrate and confirm it."*
>
> *- Jeremy Bentham*

Were you shaken like the majority of participants at our seminar? Next time you would like to eat the fattening food you love the most, start to imagine that you are eating the food that disgusts you the most. With this technique, I got rid of my worst bad habit: eating "greasy" meat. If that kind of food is written down in your answer to question #6, you won't agree with me at all. However, the decision is yours. You can experiment with this technique with any other habit.

WHILE CONTROLLING YOUR THOUGHTS, CONTROL YOUR WEIGHT

When you gain more control over your thoughts, you will shake off what I call "THE FEVER OF OVEREATING." On special cards, write down proposed suggestions and repeat them regularly until they become part of your thinking and life.

As soon as I feel hungry, or when my body gives some other sign that I want to eat, I will understand that signal instead as a clear impetus for a walk, deep breathing and drinking water. Walking, breathing and drinking water will give me much more energy than unnecessary overeating. If you act on these suggestions, you will appease the wish to overeat.

Try to remember, everything is in your mind!

HEALTH

THE DEPARTMENT OF GIVING UP SMOKING

As a nonsmoker, you may have told yourself that you could skip this chapter because it does not concern you. Of course, we congratulate you that you take such good care of your health. But I would still suggest that you read this chapter: you might be able to give somebody else some useful advice.

STOP SMOKING AND START TO BREATHE IN WITH FULL CAPACITY

Many smokers have a hard time stopping smoking because they have never taken enough time to study what they should know about their smoking habits. When I ask smokers why they smoke and why they do not stop, they give me different reasons. All of these prove that taking up smoking is caused by our emotions. Some believe that smoking relaxes them. Others are of the opinion that they will become nervous, that they will gain weight or even get a case of nerves if they stop smoking. Then, there are those who think that they do not have enough will power to stop smoking. I am not going to talk about the bad aspects of smoking, because I am sure you already know them. I will talk about the emotional reasons for smoking. In this way, it will be easier for you to give up those poisonous sticks.

SMOKING IS JUST A HABIT - A PATTERN YOU HAVE BEEN TAUGHT

When I am performing nonsmoking therapies with people who have been smoking for years, I ask them first if they are truly aware of when they smoke, when they light a cigarette. Have you ever counted how many times a day you light a cigarette?

If you smoke a pack a day, multiply the number of cigarettes in the box by the number of days in the year, and you will then get the number of cigarettes you actually smoke in a year. Next time you light a cigarette, pay attention to when or where you light it. Do you light it when you wake up? When you drink coffee? When you drive in your car? When you are relaxed at a party? When you are lonely? When you are nervous? After lunch?

Undoubtedly, you will find a predictable pattern of behavior that must be sufficiently disrupted if you want to stop smoking. With giving up smoking, I often use techniques of pain and pleasure as well as the technique of breaking up the pattern. You have repeated this behavior so many times that it has become normal for you. The habit is anchored in your nervous system.

WHY YOU STARTED SMOKING?

Remember when you lit a cigarette for the very first time? Can you also remember what happened and why that the cigarette appeared in your mouth suddenly? Did you believe that you would look more grown up and more attractive? Or were you under pressure? Did your co-worker talk you into it? My colleague told me that she started to smoke five years after an aunt passed away with whom she had really bonded. Because of one single emotionally fraught event, we are ready to poison ourselves. In addition, we do not even stop to think how beautiful life is - especially without cigarettes!

To those who ask me what I have got against smokers, the answer is, absolutely nothing. But I want you to answer one question:

Would you like your children to smoke? If you answered "no", this could be the reason that could lead you to stop smoking.

If you smoke, you probably started in adolescence. Somewhere I read that large majorities of smokers start before the age of 20, and more than half start before the age of 16. It is worth thinking about two facts: you yourself decided to start smoking, and only you yourself can decide to stop.

12 MOTIVATIONAL STEPS TOWARDS LIFE WITHOUT CIGARETTES

All the 12 steps described should be executed every day until your new identity is NON-SMOKER

1. Listen to music and relax. Tell yourself that you have accepted the final decision to stop smoking. Tell yourself that you will start NOW AND NOT TOMORROW OR NEXT YEAR. Tell yourself, "I will not smoke!" You can repeat this a few times.

2. Every day, keep repeating WHY you have stopped smoking completely.

3. Persuade yourself with the next suggestion: "I will improve my health greatly because I've stopped smoking!"

4. Keep repeating to yourself the suggestion: "I will never again purchase cigarettes, and I will always refuse if somebody offers me one."

5. Remember: the longer you abstain, the easier it will be for you to stop smoking.

6. Keep saying to yourself that you are proud for making a decision that will improve all areas in your life.

7. After each day's exercise, write down your progress. Write down how many days and months you have not been smoking.

8. Every day, keep telling yourself that no habit is stronger than the power of your thoughts.

9. Never lose hope; never become impatient; because it is for your life and health, and for the health and life of your children, if you have any.

10. Develop a substitute habit. If you stopped smoking, do something else (chew gum, exercise, breathe, commune with nature or dance). But don't exchange one bad habit for another!

11. Suggest to yourself the following idea: "Actually, I don't enjoy smoking. After all, it is only a ridiculous bad habit."

12. Make a list of all the problems smoking can cause in your health and career, and the damage it can do to your children and relationships. Write down also the advantages that non-smoking brings you. Read both lists at least twice a day.

If you follow all this advice, and if you perform all the exercises, you have made major progress in the fight against addiction, negative habits, stress, worries and insomnia.

Take note:

> "Laughter is the best medicine."
> Norman Cousins

If you want further personal growth, it is time to delve into:

SECRET #5:

THE SOURCE OF MOTIVATION

RELATIONSHIPS

"The most useful people in the world today are those men and women who can cope with each other. Human relationships are, in the educational plan of life, the most important science."

Stanley C. Allyn

IN THIS CHAPTER, YOU WILL FIND OUT:

How to forgive - forget - get healed.

☙

How to communicate effectively in private and professional life.

☙

How to deal with negative people.

☙

How to avoid students' traps.

☙

7 pieces of advice to students for more efficient study.

☙

How to raise children to become self-confident and independent.

☙

7 pieces of advice which every father or mother should master.

☙

How to find an ideal partner for a lasting relationship.

☙

How to bring in to your relationship more passion, love and understanding.

☙

How to understand your partner.

☙

How to avoid unnecessary fights which upset your love relationship.

☙

How to become the happiest husband or wife.

Until now, we have been speaking about things that concern the most important person in the world. That is you. At my seminars, I always ask: "Who do you think I am talking about when I say that we have to control relationships?" The counting starts: parents, children, colleagues, acquaintances, total strangers, and at the end I hear as well about us, about the relationship with ourselves. In this chapter, we are going to talk mostly about how to communicate effectively with people you meet in your life. We are going to talk about effective communication, which is important for success. If you would like to succeed in any aspect of the wheel of life, you have to master communication with other people. I call it communication for success. Let us see how to communicate with two people who have given you the most precious gift of all-life!

FORGIVE - FORGET - GET HEALED

You must be asking yourself now, "Whom should I forgive?" You should forgive everybody that ever hurt you. Forgiveness is a sort of remedy for different resentments that we carry in our heart towards several people we have met in our lives.

The most important people in your life you have to forgive are your parents. Of course, you can also forgive others who have hurt you in the past. Forgive and forget. People often say that they forgive their parents everything, but they still have not forgotten. Why is forgiveness so important? Because with forgiveness, you become free from all your negative emotional attachments, which are draining your creative energy. When we forgive our parents for everything, suddenly there is plenty of room in our hearts for love. We become more focused on our work, and we will succeed more easily. It does not matter how much somebody has hurt you; you must keep in mind one very important thing:

> "Let us forget and forgive injuries."
> Miguel de Cervantes

PEOPLE AREN'T THEIR DEEDS

Do not equate people with their deeds. These are two separate entities. One is the person and the other only an action that was done by that person. After you have accepted that, you will not judge people by their actions. You will not be looking at the INTENTIONS of their deeds, but you will ask for the REASONS why they do things.

> "There is only one human nature; only habits distinguish one from another."
> Confucius

When you ask yourself what somebody's INTENTION was in doing this or saying that, you put yourself in the position of a victim. You start to feel sorry for yourself. If you ask yourself what was the REASON somebody acted as he or she did, you put yourself in the position of a student who is trying to understand. Then, you are not accusing; you are learning. This thought should guide you the next time you find yourself in a conflict.

HOW I FORGAVE MY FATHER

Ever since I can remember, my communication with my father has never been positive. We did not talk much. He used to provoke me; I used to provoke him, too. I said to myself that I would never forgive him for certain things, not even on my deathbed. I was not able to talk to him cordially. I did not care. If he was not going to budge an inch, that was his concern.

IT DOESN'T HAVE TO BE LIKE THAT, OR IT'S NEVER TOO LATE

While writing this paragraph, my heart is thumping with happiness and joy. When my father celebrated his fiftieth birthday, we had our most beautiful moment together ever. Why? Because he got up, and in front of everybody told me that he was proud of me, and that he loved me. These were the words I wanted to hear more than anything in the world. These are the words every child wants to hear from his or her parents. The more often you hear these words, the better your self-image.

DON'T CHANGE OTHERS, CHANGE YOURSELF

Then, I said to myself that I could never forgive myself if I departed from this world without having a cordial conversation with my father. I decided that if he did not change, I would. I would give him my deepest, most heartfelt love and, perhaps, things would be different. I made a commitment to change my life for my father and mother, but first I had to do something for myself. Moreover, I wrote to my father.

THE LETTER OF FORGIVENESS

One evening, I sat at the table, took a sheet of paper and while listening to soft music, started to write about all the ways that my father hurt me. I wrote and wrote about whatever I could remember; tears were running down my cheeks and soaking the letter of forgiveness I was writing, which was for me a catharsis. In the end, I wrote that I forgave him for everything, I loved him, and I was happy because he gave me the most beautiful gift - life. I stuffed the letter into a drawer and left my bitter feelings behind. I felt relief in my heart, and my head became much lighter. I knew I had done the right thing.

Two weeks later, I invited all my family for lunch. I told my father - in front of everybody - what I had written down. He started to defend himself, "You must have deserved it when I spoke to you like that; it wasn't like that!" I told him that my intention was not to discuss what happened or why. I finished my "speech" with, "I just want to tell you I understand you; I love you, and I would like to have a good relationship with you. Since then, our relationship is improving every day. Now, he calls me even if it has only to ask, "Son, how are you?" "Never better," I reply.

> "He that cannot forgive others, breaks the bridge over which he himself must pass if he would ever reach heaven; for everyone has the need to be forgiven."
> - Lord Herbert

I have found out that my conclusions were correct: after I changed my way of thinking and expressed my love for him, I was given positive feedback in return. It wasn't that my father did not love me before; he just did not show it. The most beautiful moment happened when I saw my father, mother and sister at my first major motivational seminar. Then, I realized that they had started to believe in my work and in me. What's more, they even improved their own lives with the help of the advice that you are reading in this book.

HOW DRAGO FORGAVE HIS MOTHER AFTER 40 YEARS

After the motivational seminar, we met with everybody who wanted to participate in the promotion of our seminars and in spreading our mission. There were more than 100 of them! Everybody achieved incredible results within 30 days of the seminar. I was particularly moved by the story of Drago and his wife from Jesenice. Drago told me that he called his mother who had abandoned him when he was 8 years old. He kept complaining that she had not given him the necessary love. The resentment he felt was huge. After the seminar, he called her and told her that he loved her, and that he had already forgiven her for everything. "You cannot imagine what relief came over me when I hung up the phone. It was like I was reborn," he said. The relief was also visible on his face, which radiated love and warmth.

"TEARS, SINCERITY AND FORGIVENESS OVERFLOWED IN THE HOUSE"

A few hours ago, I met a group of children who had been invited by our company for a week of holidays to learn the skills of scouting, love, forgiveness, setting goals in their lives and many other things that are described in this book. The group was something special. These were children who did not get love from their parents; they grew up in families with physical abuse, sleepless nights, and life under constant pressure. That is why they found shelter for themselves in the House for Youth. For two hours, I talked to Andrej, Darja, Marjan, Marko, Blanka, Andrej, Suzana, Gregor, Denis, Renata, Lidija, Mihaela, Sebastijan and Branko about the significance of forgiving their parents for what they had done to them.

I talked about the meaning of life and told them that their future was now in their hands. The most precious gift was given to them - life; now they had to decide for themselves what to do with it. The tears of hope in their eyes really moved me. They sparkled with new life. As I write this part of the book, it is 10.30 p.m., and I have just received a message on the mobile phone from Bogdan, from the House for Youth, who wrote: "TEARS, SINCERITY AND FORGIVENESS OVERFLOWED IN THE HOUSE. THANKS."

I am certain that the lives of these children, after this meeting, will never be the same. Thanks are due to Andreja, Roman and Bogdan, who unselfishly shared their precious time with these children who need hope and somebody to understand them. I strongly believe that those seven days will be crucial for their development.

STOP BLAMING OTHERS FOR YOUR OWN FAILURES

Until the age of 25, I always said that my mother and father were to blame for my failure to achieve something more in my life. I put the blame on society, government, laws and other people; I criticized everyone. I was sure that everybody else was to blame for the life I was living. Then, I decided to take control of my destiny. I sat in the pilot's seat and became the pilot of my own plane with, "Smiljan; you are 25 years old, and since the age of 18, you've had your I.D. and passport, so you are independent and fully responsible for your life." I recommend that you, too, take your passport and cross the borders of self-pity to find the luck, happiness and success, which are waiting for you. You only have to find out where to look for them. For happiness, contentment and wealth, there are no borders; there are just borders that you set up in your mind. Forgive, take responsibility for your life and run toward happiness and success.

> "Nobody can forgive me except myself."
> - Ding Ling

THE DEPARTMENT OF EFFECTIVE COMMUNICATION

THE ART OF COMMUNICATION

How to communicate is one of the biggest challenges that we face in companies, society and among ourselves. In my company, I also use a technique of communication that is called "the bridge of communication." It is a technique we can use for effective communication, and with which we can avoid many problems and much pain and misunderstanding. I often hear things such as "I didn't say that," "I didn't think like that," "you didn't understand me correctly," "that is not true," "who said that?" "I don't know why you are like that," "now you've hurt me", and so forth. Do you ever communicate like this? The way we communicate with others largely determines success in our lives.

Bad communication is the biggest weakness in the operational system of certain companies. That is why, in every company that invites me to meet with their employees, I talk about interpersonal communication.

> "A good listener is not only popular everywhere, but after a while he begins to know something."
> Wilson Mizner

After you use the technique I will explain to you, and incorporate it into your personal and professional lives, you will increase the quality of your life as well as success in your work.

First, let us look at:

WHY DO WE COMMUNICATE? WHAT IS THE INTENTION OF COMMUNICATION?

With communication, we usually try to achieve 4 goals. We strive to:

1. Feel positive emotions.
2. Increase the positive emotions we already feel.

3. Eliminate negative emotions.
4. Realize our goals.

However, the basic reason we communicate is to FEEL GOOD. When I ask the participants at the seminar why they communicate, different answers emerge. Some communicate because they must; others say that communicating is a pleasure for them. The third group says that they could not live without communication. Many more are communicating to earn money. The answers certainly do vary.

FIND OUT HOW YOU COMMUNICATE IN STRESSFUL SITUATIONS

Under genuine stress, each person communicates in his or her own way. To find out how you communicate in a stressful situation, complete the next exercise:

EXERCISE 28

1. Under stress I usually communicate so that...

___

2. If I want to persuade somebody, I usually communicate so that...

___

3. When I'm under stress, the other person usually sees me as...

___

4. How do you see me when I am under stress and communicate with you?

___

___

I recommend that you do this exercise at work, in your company, or within the circle of your family. You will see how much fun it is. Do not get upset with the answers given by others to the 4th question.

After we have done this exercise within a company, we see work related results change.

THE BELIEFS WE NEED TO COMMUNICATE MORE EASILY WITH OTHERS:

1. People are not their beliefs.
2. People always give as much as they can.
3. There are always two sides to a story.
4. More important than people's behavior is who they really are.

NEVER MAKE ASSUMPTIONS ABOUT WHAT HAPPENED

One day, the president of a large Insurance Company called me. He told me that my colleague had made a serious mistake. When I heard this, I thought that I would explode with anger at her. But before I said anything, and perhaps wrongfully accused someone who otherwise was really doing a good job, I decided to have a talk with her. I prepared the conversation by asking myself 7 questions.

TEST OF THE TRUTH: 7 QUESTIONS THAT YOU ASK YOURSELF BEFORE YOU COMMUNICATE WITH SOMEONE WHO HAS UPSET YOU

1. Am I ready to learn something new? Am I ready to do something to improve the situation? Would this person help me, even if I show that he or she is wrong? Will I improve after this conversation?

2. What really disturbed me about this situation? What significance do I give to what happened?

3. Is it possible that I am mistaken about what has happened? Do I have all the information to help me understand precisely what I want to talk about?

4. Could this situation be interpreted differently?

5. What do I have to do to feel better? (Find another interpretation, find more information, understand his or her position, know that this person likes me, change the working pattern, apologize to this person, remember that I like him or her, think of how we used to understand and get along with each other well).

6. What can I do to communicate well with this person to improve matters in the future?

7. Am I going to create a stronger bond with this person after our conversation?

All these questions were considered, and then I talked to her with a completely different attitude. I found out that, in fact, her intentions were entirely different from how they had been represented to me, but that faulty communication had resulted in a misunderstanding. I would have done serious damage to our relationship if I had accused her immediately without asking myself these questions.

INSTEAD OF ACCUSING PEOPLE, BUILD A BRIDGE OF COMMUNICATION

Get rid of stress. Say, "I'm sorry that I'm somewhat upset. I know what kind of person you are, and I know that you wouldn't deliberately do such a thing. I would just like to understand what you were trying to achieve when you said that and/ or acted in this way. I need your input to help me to understand what happened.

> "A basic rule in human life is that a kind appearance triggers a kind reaction."
> - Jawaharlal Nehru

- Ask for an explanation - don't accuse.

After this kind of approach, any further discussion will definitely be more fruitful. How do you solve communication problems in your own company? There are two common mistaken ways of solving problems with communication at home and in the workplace:

a) We carry the problems within ourselves.

or

b) We accuse others, complain and, in fact, complicate the problems.

Neither the first nor the second way leads to better communication and cooperation, but both will certainly ruin relations between employees and among the people with whom we are in constant daily contact.

HOW TO DEAL WITH NEGATIVE PEOPLE

Years ago, when I began a career in sales for the first time, I started to meet with rejections and excuses from clients. It upset me that people did not understand or accept what I was talking about. At the time, I did not know that their excuses or negative remarks actually signified a cry for help.

> "We cannot avoid relatives and physical characteristics, because we inherit them. Friends and clothes we can choose, so we should be careful to find those which suit us."
> Volney Streamer

Today, I know that any excuses that clients come up with are actually requests for more information. This is how I explain this particular reaction from the perspective of a client: "According to the information which has so far been given to me, I'm not interested in your product. If you give me more information, I might consider buying it." From my experience, I can tell that most clients say no about five times before they decide to say yes. The job of a salesperson is to inform clients about the product he or she is selling, and to give information to convince them they need the product, and that it will fulfill their expectations. If they tell me they have to think it over, I know they still have many questions that I will have to answer.

NEGATIVE PEOPLE ARE ACTUALLY ASKING FOR HELP

Why am I talking about sales techniques in the passage on how to deal with negative people? I am dealing with this area because in sales you are constantly dealing with negative people. You have to convince a customer to buy a product; you have to convince "negative" people to be positive. You also have to know that negative people usually do not have the best self-image; they are not self-confident and sure of themselves. Forget their negative words and actions. These people are so uncertain and frightened inside, that this is how they keep their distance from others in order to feel safe. Actually, they are asking for help.

Another type of person you encounter in sales is the one full of self-praise. They do this because they are not completely sure of themselves, and they need confirmation. If they do not get this from others, they make sure that their ego is fed by praising themselves.

> "Chance makes our parents, but choice makes our friends."
> - Jacques Delille

The only way you can help negative people is to deposit something into THEIR ACCOUNT OF SELF-CONFIDENCE. When such a person complains or criticizes, try to remember him or her by successes or "good moments" and give praise. Ask yourself what you could do to help them build self-confidence. If you have a colleague who is like that, look for the smallest opportunities to give praise. That will give this person the feeling of being worthy of something.

At my seminars, by observing body language, I can spot those who tend to be negative. They often sit with crossed legs and arms, and there are no smiles on their faces. After a while, they start to open up and cooperate. After a seminar, they often come and tell me that they did not want to come, but that they did because their superior asked them to attend. But it is a pleasure when they tell me that they enjoyed it, and that they learned many useful things despite their initial skepticism.

> *"A man on his way through life always meets those who help him to grow and develop."*
> — Anonymous

If you find yourself spending a lot of time with negative people, I suggest the following:

1. Think about your own inclinations. We often attract in our lives people who are like us.
2. Take the initiative and change yourself first - you will be surprised what will happen with your "negative friends." Gradually, they will start to change, too. Nevertheless, be patient: this process can take a while!
3. Surround yourself with a protective circle of people who have a positive effect on you.
4. Put up with people's negative inclinations and stop complaining.

ATTITUDE TOWARD SCHOOL AND STUDY

7 ADVICE FOR STUDENTS, AND FOR THOSE WHO WOULD LIKE TO ACHIEVE MORE

I am often invited to high schools where I talk about motivation for studying, attitudes towards studying and life in general. I also talk about motivation for work after studies have been completed. At the secondary school of economics in Maribor, over 100 pupils and seven of their professors were assembled. We really had a good time. After these kinds of lectures, I often receive inspirational notes from students who need the kind of advice I am giving the most. At my lecture, I provide them with some easy to use advice that I have accumulated while studying myself. Let us see if it can be of any use to you, whether you are a student or a parent who would like to motivate a child to study. Give your child this book to read independently. You will be surprised at the result!

TIP #1
STUDY EVEN THOUGH YOU DON'T THINK YOU WILL EVER NEED THE KNOWLEDGE YOU ARE BEING TAUGHT

The job at which I am employed right now has almost nothing in common with my education. I graduated from the Faculty of Law in Ljubljana, after which I worked as a trainee at the High Court. Even then, I used to ask myself why I was studying certain materials if I did not intend to work in that field.

Today, I know why I was studying. First, I studied to get a general education and that definitely that was one stage in my personal growth. Yet, the benefits of such study were revealed later. Five years ago, when I wanted to register my first company, there were certain conditions for that: a minimum of secondary school and four years of working experience, or a university degree and one year of working experience. The condition for four years of working experience I did not fulfill, but I did have one year of work experience and a university degree. It was lucky that I had graduated on time, otherwise I would not have been able immediately to do the work of which I am so proud and at which I have learned so much.

I HATE TYPING

In the secondary school for policemen, we took typing as an obligatory subject. We studied typing on old typewriters. In the belief that typing was not a "masculine" skill, I rejected that subject totally. "Thank God that I can type", I said to myself a while ago when I decided to write this book. Now, I can type day and night without checking the keyboard. What luck, otherwise this book would have taken years to write! You cannot tell how you will eventually use the knowledge you are learning, so give your best effort to your studies today.

TIP #2
WHEN YOU GRADUATE, THAT DOESN'T MEAN THAT YOU WILL BE WEALTHY, HAPPY AND CONTENTED

Your education is only a ticket to the labor market, a market of demands and requests, the market of success or failure. It is like purchasing a ticket to board a train. It's up to you to choose where to sit, or even to decide if you are going to sit at all. Do not give up and jump off at the next station if you cannot find an available seat right away. It is not like a plane flight where they book a seat for you. Here, you have to fight for a good seat. In order for your train journey to be as comfortable as possible, I suggest that you absorb the knowledge written in this and other books about personal growth. You also should consider the following:

TIP #3
GET A PART-TIME JOB

By getting part-time jobs, you will gain experience in different fields; you will meet people from different companies, and if you prove yourself, they might invite you to join them. You will definitely have an advantage over those who are not familiar with the company. By performing part time (student) work, you acquire working habits and some necessary self-confidence. I always ask students if they have any work experience. Can you imagine somebody who comes to your company at the age of 25 to ask for a job who does not have any work experience? Of course, you should not neglect your studies because you need work experience. My friend Matej earned all of his own money for his studies, and on top of that he was a model student.

TIP #4
KEEP EDUCATING YOURSELF AFTER GRADUATION

After finishing formal education, the majority of people get a job and then neglect their personal development. But if you are holding this book, you must be one of those who want something more from life.

TIP #5
SET GOALS

The most important chapter in this book is the one on goals. If you have not done the exercises, do them now. When I asked 100 pupils to raise their hands if they had clear, written goals for their future, I did not see any hands. Just after that, I asked them how many of them wanted to be wealthy, successful and contented - and suddenly I saw 200 hands. This will not lead to success! It is like trying to build a house without any plans.

TIP #6
TELL ME WITH WHOM YOU ASSOCIATE, AND I WILL TELL YOU WHO YOU ARE

85% of the success that you will achieve in your life depends on your associates. It is not that they are responsible for your life; you are responsible for it and for deciding who will be among the 85%. If we associate with people who have lower standards, aims and goals than we do, we will not be very ambitious. We will even lower our standards in order to get closer to such mediocre people, otherwise we could lose their admiration. Choose your associates carefully. Let your friends and acquaintances motivate you, encourage and support you, but not hold you back or demoralize you.

> "With whom you associate depends on what you will become. The quality of human life is indirectly dependent on the expectations of the people with whom you associate. Choose your friends very carefully."
>
> - Anthony Robbins

Write out a 7th tip yourself! Send me your ideas. I will be glad to put them in my next book.

TIP #7
BEWARE OF TOO MUCH PARTYING AND PROCRASTINATION

Sorry! You will have to write TIP #8 because just now Alenka, a third-year student at the Pedagogical Faculty, came into my office. Her advice is golden. I do not know why I did not remember it myself. Probably, I did not want to admit it. The years of studying are sweet. That is when you travel, have fun and meet people, but it is also dangerous if you are caught up in parties that never end. Days, weeks, months (and years) pass quickly, and suddenly it is examination time. Moreover, final exams come at the most beautiful time of the year. "Oh, I will take the next one, in the fall," is the most common excuse that I hear and have used myself. I passed almost all my exams the first time. Then, there came the last exam, which I had delayed for nearly a year. Today, I know why. I was afraid of the new phase in my life I was about to enter, which was finding a job and working for a living. Suddenly, you are responsible, and you have to make money to survive. That period definitely signals a turning point for each of us. Do not delay your examinations, or your graduation diploma because if you do, you are missing wonderful opportunities for further development.

THE DEPARTMENT OF RAISING SELF-CONFIDENT AND INDEPENDENT CHILDREN

7 TIPS ON HOW TO HELP A CHILD TO GAIN SELF-CONFIDENCE AND SUCCESS

I can hear your questions: "Do you have any children? How dare you give advice on this subject if you are childless?" Although I do not have children, I have learned a lot from experience. How? Do you really want to know? It is because we both were children once. Our memories of childhood are the most valuable experiences. Although I do not yet have children of my own (I am, however, the godfather to Kevin, Brina and Tanja), many people ask me how to raise their children. I am glad to give them advice, because I know the behavior of both grown-up people and children. Adults are nothing more than grown-up children.

TIP#1
BE A ROLE MODEL

It is hard to tell a child not to smoke because it is not healthy if you are smoking yourself. It is almost impossible to forbid him to drink alcohol if you drink it too. It is hard to stop him cursing if he can hear such language from you practically every day. You cannot forbid him to watch TV because you would like to watch your favorite soap opera. You are a child's major role model, for most of his or her whole life. By the way, if you look at yourself in the mirror, what will you see? Yourself. You have to be aware that in the years of development, you are the mirror for your child. He or she will see your image long after launching out in life. If there is something about your child that you do not like very much, you have to ask yourself where it was learned.

Perhaps you are bothered by exactly the same things reflected in your child's behavior that you would like to change in yourself. You may have not succeeded in making these changes. Now, however, you would like to see these changes in your child. is hard to tell a child not to smoke because it is not healthy if you are smoking yourself. It is almost impossible to forbid him to drink alcohol if you drink it too. It is hard to stop him cursing if he can hear such language from you almost every day. You cannot forbid him to watch TV because you would like to watch your favorite soap opera. You are a child's major role model, for most of his or her whole life. By the way, if you look at yourself in the mirror, what will you see?

Yourself. You have to be aware that in the years of development, you are the mirror for your child. He or she will see your image long after launching out in life. If there is something about your child that you do not like very much, you have to ask yourself where it was learned. Perhaps you are bothered by exactly the same things reflected in your child's behavior that you would like to change in yourself. You may have not succeeded in making these changes. Now, however, you would like to see these changes in your child.

TIP #2
DON'T COMPARE YOUR CHILD WITH OTHERS

I frequently hear parents say to their children, "You are exactly like your father, mother, sister, or like someone on TV." That definitely is not good for the self-image of your child. By comparing him to others, you do not allow him to develop his own personality. On the other hand, it is unfair to a child to tell him that he should be like his sister, brother or friend, because that is not who he is. Children have their own personalities, just like adults. Tell your relatives not to compare your child with others. Allow him or her to develop a unique personality.

TIP #3
LIMIT TV TIME

Do you remember the chapter where I discussed how much negative information we received in early childhood? Much of this negative information we get through television, radio, newspapers and magazines. In our childhood, TV is our ELECTRONIC REDUCER OF OPTIMISM; when we grow up, it changes into an ELECTRONIC REDUCER OF MONEY. At my seminars, I often ask, "How much does TV cost you?" Most of the participants mention an amount they paid for a new TV set or for the monthly cable bill. When I tell them that TV costs them over $25,000 yearly, they look at me in surprise.

I offer these supporting arguments: calculate the time you spend in front of the TV, when you are not watching anything important, or learning anything new. Carefully choose the shows your child is going to watch. Let them be mostly educational ones.

TIP #4
REMEMBER THAT A CHILD CANNOT BE PERFECT

Sometimes you find yourself thinking that your child could behave in a more mature manner, and you might even tell him that. On the other hand, you treat him like a child. This can be confusing for you both. Although he might sometimes be behaving well, most likely is not going to be consistent. Tell him instead that you are not perfect either, and do not criticize him constantly — that won't help.

TIP #5
ENCOURAGE YOUR CHILD TO READ AND TO WATCH EDUCATIONAL MOVIES

The easiest way to do this is to visit a bookshop together. Go into a bookshop and together choose the books they find most interesting. Let them read books about heroes who overcame fear and uncertainty. Maybe these are not the most educational ones, but they will certainly give them a lot of self-confidence, which they will need later when they face similar decisions in life. I can still remember the books I used to read as a child. Some of them were very educational, and I still use them at seminars. While the child is reading a book or watching TV, help him or her to understand the meaning of what is read or seen.

TIP #6
TELL YOUR CHILD OFTEN OF YOUR LOVE

When I speak with children and young adults, they tell me that they miss the hugs of their loved ones and friends. Praise a child often, and tell him that you love him. Let him know this also with a hug or a pat on the shoulder. Do not be ashamed to express sincere love. Do not criticize him; criticize his actions. If he has done something wrong, tell him that you still love him, and that you always will. After that, tell him what you did not like, and explain what he should be doing instead. Don't go on the attack, saying things like, "You're clumsy," "I knew you wouldn't make it," "you are just like...," "go and watch TV," "you can't do anything anyhow."

TIP #7
TEACH CHILDREN INDEPENDENCE

You will often find yourself in a situation in which you could do some things much faster than your child. Be patient. If you always do everything for him, he will become (and remain) very dependent; he will have a hard time finding a job, and getting into new ventures; he will not be able to travel by himself or make difficult decisions. Undoubtedly, you do not want him to be dependent on you all his life. I am sure that you wish your child to grow up to be an independent, courageous and brave person. Only by encouraging your child to be independent will he or she be able to survive in today's competitive world.

THE DEPARTMENT OF LOVE

ARE YOU STILL SINGLE? HOW TO FIND AN IDEAL PARTNER

Many people are of the opinion that they do not need a partner in order to be happy. That is perfectly fine if they live by themselves. Yet, the need for love is one of the most basic human needs. If we do not satisfy that need, it will be hard to be completely happy. We are happy if somebody loves us and supports us. We like the feeling that somebody cares about us, that we are not alone; we like security. If you hear somebody saying that he does not want another relationship because all men or women are the same, it is just because he or she does not want to be disappointed again. People who were disappointed in one relationship do not want to go through the same pain again.

They are comparing THIS and THAT, but you already know that THIS and THAT are not THE SAME. I can assure you that you can find an "ideal" partner, but only if you have a clear vision of what you want. It is the same with goals. You have to choose a partner carefully because we are talking here about a long-term relationship that will have a major impact on your life."

EXERCISE 28

1. WHAT DO YOU EXPECT AND HOPE FOR FROM YOUR FUTURE PARTNER?

Write down everything that comes to mind, because you will then know where to focus.

Write your list of desirable characteristics in descending order (from the most important to the least important).

_____
_____
_____
_____
_____
_____

In this exercise, you should bear in mind that your future partner is only human and that nobody is perfect. (Think of how others might describe you!)

2. WRITE DOWN THE FEATURES YOU WOULDN'T LIKE AT ALL IN A PARTNER

Write the list of undesirable characteristics in descending order (the first one is the least undesirable one)

_____
_____
_____
_____
_____
_____

3. WHAT KIND OF PERSON SHOULD I BECOME TO ATTRACT A PERSON LIKE THAT INTO MY LIFE?

This is the most important question. Take a piece of paper to answer. Of course, you must know that it will be very hard to get 100% of everything you wish for. If you get 70%, you should be very satisfied. The remaining 30% you will gain through learning to compromise in your relationship.

HOW TO WEATHER LIFE'S UPS AND DOWNS WITH YOUR PARTNER

Even if you do not yet have a partner, do not skip this chapter. Read it for the future.

There are many excellent books about how to establish wonderful relationships with a partner. You know many things already, but you do not act on what you know. Just think how it was when you were getting to know your husband or wife-to-be. What did you talk about with him/her? Where did you take him/her? What wonderful things did you do or experience?

> "Do not waste time with useless hatred, and do not compete for who is going to sulk the most."
> Samuel Johnson

Metka and Franci were attending our seminar. Their marriage was just about to fall apart. They had been married for nearly thirty years. They had a nice life, had raised two children, built a house, bought a good car, and built one cottage on the coast and one in the mountains. When they could finally enjoy the fruits of their work and dedicate all their love to each other, their relationship started to fall apart. After the seminar, I received a letter from them in which they wrote that they realized why their relationship was worsening each year. It touched them the most when I talked about the comfort zone and setting goals. They discovered that they had felt passion, excitement and love when they still had common goals about which they used to dream, but after they made these come true, love suddenly vanished. They no longer talked about their common plans; they did not dream together. They had all the material goods they wanted; their children had grown up, but they had lost the compass that had led them ahead in their shared life. After the seminar, they set new common goals for the next thirty years of their lives, and now they are facing the future with a great deal of optimism.

I am sure it is similar with many couples who find themselves at a crisis in their relationship, when and if they no longer have common goals. The solution? Through talking, couples must reset the way in which they will direct their goals.

WHY DIVORCE HAPPENS AND HOW TO AVOID IT

Each of us has rules - conscious or unconscious - about what a partner must and must not do. Finish the following sentences; you may find out what your own rules are.

EXERCISE 30

Each of us has rules - conscious or unconscious - about what a partner must and must not do. Finish the following sentences; you may find out what your own rules are.

He(She) has to:_____

He(She) cannot:_____

He(She) can never:_____

He(She) always has to:_____

He(She) should:_____
He(She) shouldn't:_____
He(She) should never:_____
He(She) should always:_____

If he(she) loves me, then he(she) will_____
If he(she) loves me, then he(she) will not_____

Rules which contain HAS TO or HE (SHE) CANNOT are always the most important rules. To break them might cause divorce.

Answer the following questions separately from your partner, then review them and comment on them together.

1. What do I wish for the most? What is it that he (she) must do and what must he (she) never do?

_____
_____
_____

2. What are the needs of my partner? What do I have to do in order to keep my partner satisfied?

_____
_____
_____

When you have answered these questions with your partner and discussed them openly, it could mean a new start in a shared life for you.

Often, disillusioned women or men call me who are just on the verge of divorce. They ask me why this happened to them, when they have tried to be good spouses. To answer this question is not easy, but if they ask, I tell them honestly, "You are in this situation because you didn't try hard enough, because you didn't give to the relationship everything that you could. Maybe you were giving 100% in other fields, but not in the area of your relationship."

Also, be aware that your relationship could be more passionate if you gave more - unreservedly.

EXERCISE 31

In the following seven days, keep testing everything written above concerning the Department of Love. You are going to be thrilled with the improvement in the quality of your relationship with your partner. These seven days could undoubtedly be prolonged over many days, weeks, months or years - because you will find out immediately how fully you will start to enjoy life.

If you suffer from lack of motivation, read Secret Number 6.

SECRET #6:

THE FUEL OF MOTIVATION

EMOTIONAL STRATEGIES FOR MOTIVATION

"Action and reaction, ebb and flow, trial and error, change - this is the rhythm of living. Out of our overconfidence, fear, out of our fear, clear vision and fresh hope. And out of hope, progress."

Bruce Barton

IN THIS CHAPTER, YOU WILL FIND OUT:

Why motivAction and not motivation.

ଓଃ

How you can motivate yourself with the help of two forces that determine human life - the power of pain and pleasure.

ଓଃ

How to increase motivation for top achievements radically and immediately.

ଓଃ

7 strategies of motivation including physical and emotional strategies of motivation.

ଓଃ

Strategies of mental motivation.

ଓଃ

How to become motivated, determined and self-confident with a snap of the fingers.

ଓଃ

How to maintain permanent motivation for achievement of your goals.

ଓଃ

How to make a "recipe for permanent motivation."

NEW APPROACHES TO MOTIVATION

Today, executives are not sufficiently aware that their employees are emotional beings with needs, wishes and goals. Managers are often unaware that their employees have certain fears, worries and limiting beliefs that block them in their personal happiness and influence effectiveness in the workplace. Many times, employees return from seminars and workshops with the thought, "I've spent a useless day at a seminar trying to motivate me to be a better employee." There are only a few leaders who are aware that an effective employee is an employee who is happy, even in his life. However, the fact is that an employee spends one-third of his life at work, so it should not be a matter of indifference how much pleasure his life is bringing him.

I keep noticing that people in the workplace behave much as they do at home. The same patterns of thinking, the same fears, doubts and worries that they have in their personal life are reflected in the workplace. Let us take the example of an employee who had difficulties making contact with new people, even in his private life. Such a person will have similar problems establishing cordial contact with employees and with customers of the company. There is also the question of communication over the phone. Moreover, the employees who are introverted will not be open to change in the company. They will hang on to routine procedures and avoid new ones that could move them out of their comfort zones.

The goal of modern companies should not be the constant motivation of employees through various financial incentives, but rather through motivation on the emotional level. What would you say if I told you that you could motivate your employees with a snap of your fingers? What would you give to your employees to be motivated even when you are not present? Think how wonderful it would be if your employees could motivate themselves constantly? This is what this chapter is about. How can you motivate yourself with the help of tools you already have, but have not used until now? These are new, revolutionary techniques of motivation for top achievement. When you integrate them into your life, you will achieve excellent results.

Financial motivation is short-term motivation; it is emotions that make a person keep going. Today, you can encourage employees much more through various forms of education, where, besides professional skills, they will also gain the skills that they need for a happier and more contented personal life. They have to be educated in what is called 'soft' knowledge. Consequently, they have to master techniques for relaxing, strategies for motivating themselves, solving problems and ways of communication with employees and others. They have to learn how to get rid of fears and doubts, how to deal correctly with their finances, how to plan their work and leisure life and how to set priorities. Moreover, employees need to master how to distinguish the important from the unimportant in life and how, through better nutrition, they can increase their well-being and thus achieve greater personal and professional effectiveness.

Many leading companies are now facing the challenge of encouraging their managers to take care of their health because they are constantly under stress. The fast pace of life demands that they eat quickly, which can, in the long run, have negative consequences for their health and, ultimately, for the welfare of the company. We have to ask what happens when a leading associate leaves the company because of unnecessary health problems for a long period. An employee may well face this possibility and other problems today, in order to survive in the effort to harmonize the demands of the company with those of his family.

NOT MOTIVATION BUT MOTIVACTION

Each of us has the power within to overcome major fears and limiting beliefs. Many people often say that they cannot change or solve certain problems and habits (for example: smoking, overeating, gambling, shopping, procrastination) because they do not have enough knowledge and will to do so. I agree with those who believe that you must acquire sufficient knowledge to allow for change and development in your life, but I disagree with those who are invoking the lack of both as an excuse for inactivity.

> "God gives nothing to those who keep their arms crossed."
> - Bam Bara (West African proverb)

The only thing that controls human behavior is MOTIVACTION. You have read correctly, motivAction. Where does this expression come from? A while ago, I was invited to the secondary school of economics, where I spoke to fourth graders about motivation. When I was sitting in front of the computer the previous evening and deciding what to tell them about motivation, the miraculous word that can push all people towards achievement appeared in front of my eyes. I was enlightened: MOTIVATION is only temporary and vanishes fast if we do not take concrete action! ACTION is what takes motivation further. No wonder that so many people are motivated only for a while, and then they fall back into the condition they were in before. If you would like to be constantly motivated you have to have a specific MOTIVE for your goals and achievements, but you also have to act - ACTION is what gives you strength.

> "The secret of success is learning how to use pain and pleasure instead of having pain and pleasure use you. If you do that, you're in control of your life. If you don't, life controls you."
> Anthony Robbins

THE POWER OF THE PAIN AND THE PLEASURE - TECHNIQUE NAC (Neuro Associative Conditioning)*

MotivAction depends on two forces that direct human behavior. These are:

1. The fear of pain or the need to avoid pain.
2. The desire for comfort or pleasure.

However, in general, people do more to avoid pain than to feel pleasure. That is one of the main reasons why people stay paralyzed because of various fears. People who are successful have managed triumphantly to overcome their fears and doubts and have developed a series of positive beliefs that maintain them in a positive mental state. So, you can think that you are capable of doing something, or you are not capable of doing something - in both cases, you are right. Everything you believe in can become true. If you would like to change a certain behavior or limiting belief, all you have to do is to associate the old belief

---

*Anthony Robbins; Awaken the Giant Within

with pain, and pleasure or comfort with a new belief. Before we learn how to banish forever your fears and self-destructive and limiting beliefs, we will find out which actions trigger specific emotions.

MOTIVATION, ENTHUSIASM, ENERGY

MOTIVATION WITHOUT ACTION means nothing. Having goals, ideas and plans means nothing if we do not have the motivation or energy to achieve these goals.

Motivation is, in essence, energy for action that will lead us closer to our goals. The level of your motivation will affect everything you do in your life. How you are motivated determines your work efficiency. If you are a salesperson, your motivation determines how many sales calls you are going to make and how successful your presentations are going to be. If you are a manager of a company, your motivation will determine how you treat people and how successful your team or company is. Motivation also determines how passionate your relationships with your partner and your children are. What if you were still as motivated as you were in the first three months of your relationship? Would things be different? I am sure they would. So, it will not come as a surprise that participants in my seminar on motivation subsequently dramatically change relationships with their families and in the workplace. It's all because of motivation! Ivo and Ana were attending one of my first seminars on motivation. Ivo was a successful businessman who, because he was working so hard, forgot the law of give and take. That day, while they were driving to the seminar, he was complaining that it did not make sense to attend seminars because they were waste of time and money.

After the seminar, I received a letter from his daughter, in which she wrote that just two weeks after the seminar she and her mother were crying tears of joy. Why? A change occurred because her father fell in love with her mother again. He talked with them much more and, for the first time in a while, there were roses on the table, signifying his love. What a change that was in a family that had everything except love and respect!

If you are an athlete, success depends on the motivation that you achieve at competitions. Because sports organizations are increasingly becoming aware of this, they invited me to participate in motivating the Slovene ski team.

I do hope that you already understand the importance of motivation in every field. Sometimes, I make a joke and say that it also takes motivation to get out of bed in the morning. Judging for myself, that is very true. When I was working in the police force, it took me half an hour to get out of bed and go to work. Now, when I am doing what I love, and it brings me so much pleasure, I am already looking forward to going to work the night before.

When I analyzed the salesmen in my company, I found that motivated salesmen are on average 15% more successful. Can you imagine what would happen if you or your salesmen were motivated an additional 15%? By how much do you think your own sales would jump, and the sales of the whole company? With motivation, everything is possible!

THE MOTIVATION SCALE

Before you encounter the tools for short-term and long-term motivation, we are going to see how you can measure the level of the motivation that affects your efficiency. There are many ways to measure motivation; the method described here is very simple, and you can use it at any time. You have to ask yourself the question, "Where am I on the motivation scale from 0 to 10?"

- 0   1   2   3   4   5   6   7   8   9   10   -

If you are at level 1, it means that you are as motivated as an old engine that has been in the museum for the last thirty years. If you are at level 10, you are ready to take big steps toward your goal. Perhaps you will say that it is very hard to maintain level 10 all the time. However, nobody says that you have to be at level 10; you can be at level 11, if you want. The peak of motivation does not mean that you are jumping around and going crazy, although movement and screaming are among the main EMOTIONAL STRATEGIES OF MOTIVATION, as I call them. You can be motivated and calm in the arms of your beloved! Most of the time, you are going to be between 3 and 7.

Ask yourself where you are on the motivation scale from 1 to 10 at this moment. Remember where you are, because you are going to do another test. Of course, the level of motivation will be affected by many external and internal factors. You will learn how to utilize these for your benefit.

3 BASIC FACTORS ON WHICH YOUR MOTIVATION DEPENDS

As soon as you know where you are on the motivation scale and where you would like to be, all the rest is simple. You have to use the strategies of motivation that I will describe further on.

1. NUTRITION

More about the importance of nutrition can be read in the chapter about health, but it would not be amiss if I remind you again how crucial nutrition is for your motivation and for the level of energy in your body. Remember how you feel after a heavy lunch: eating a steak, potatoes, salad, fruit, dessert, and then drinking coffee and maybe lighting a cigarette. You feel drowsy and want to sleep! Clearly, proper nutrition is important in staying energetic and motivated.

2. PHYSICAL ACTIVITY

If you choose to be a couch potato, you can hardly congratulate yourself for being motivated, because motivation means a constant flood of mental and physical energy. For high motivation, it is not necessary to be a top athlete, but it is imperative that you work out at least 3 times a week. If you can manage more, it can only be to your benefit.

3. ENOUGH REST AND SLEEP

Do you remember the mood at work the morning after a big party? You and your colleagues were not even in the mood to talk because of hangovers and sleeplessness. I suggest that for better efficiency, you charge your batteries regularly with enough rest and sleep.

7 PHYSICAL STRATEGIES OF MOTIVATION

The strategies that I am about to describe can be used at any time. Everything you are going to read; however, you have to test for yourself; otherwise, you will not feel the impact that these strategies can have in increasing your motivation.

1. THE MOTIVATIONAL GESTURE

What is the motivational gesture? Actually, you are using it already, only you are not aware of it. These motivational gestures are evident in athletes when they are trying to achieve a fantastic result, such as setting a record or scoring a basket or a goal. At that time, they use their body in a very specific way: they clench their fists, clap in certain ways and speak positive words to themselves. All of that is part of their strategy for motivation. Some of them are not even aware of what they are doing but, despite that, they instinctively know how to motivate themselves before the important test. If that works for sportsmen, why shouldn't it for you? You will find out how to do this yourself in the chapter about anchoring (NLP), which I always demonstrate in my motivational seminar. When the Slovene basketball player, Milo, came to me without energy, we went through the process of anchoring. After a few minutes of work, he was sweating as if he had been at practice. Why? Because he used all his senses in becoming anchored and, with the help of motivational gestures, he relived the feelings of victory. Since then, he has regained energy, and what is more important, has achieved access to these sources of power, self-confidence, determination and motivation. Because of these positive results, our seminars are successful. We show people strategies for motivation, which they can use by themselves to achieve fantastic results.

Sudden, fast, strong gestures can instantly increase the level of your motivation because they automatically speed up your heart beat and speed up your breathing thus allowing greater circulation of blood and increased oxygen in your body and brain.

Fast clapping, snapping the fingers, beating the chest, jumping up and down, and clenching your fists are all signs of victory; all of these gestures are tools with which you can instantly increase the level of your motivation. Seminar participants nowadays try strategies of motivation on themselves. The result: despite all day activity, jumping and other physical exertions, they look rejuvenated after ten hours. In this way, during the whole seminar, we are training our nervous system to be in excellent condition. Nevertheless, it's like making the effort to stay fit. You cannot get muscles if you lift a weight only once. If you want to maintain muscle mass, you must work out; if you would like to increase muscle mass, you have to work out beyond your comfort zone. If you want everything that this book talks about to become a part of your life, you have to exercise and practice the techniques constantly. You have to practice at least 30 days in a row — then it becomes a habit.

EXERCISE 32

Get up and move your hands away from your body. Now, very s l o w l y clap with both hands. Repeat this five times. How do you feel? I can bet that the level of your energy fell and with it also your motivation.

Now do the exercise so that you clap at full speed, strength and energy. Do you feel the difference? Absolutely! Exercise, you will not be sorry!

2. THE MOTIVATIONAL INHALE

EXERCISE 33

Do this exercise as well. Breathe in deeply and for a few seconds hold your breath, then strongly exhale. Repeat this five times with increasing speed. How do you feel? Do you feel dizzy?

The motivational inhale can give you strength and energy for almost 30 minutes. Try to use the motivational gesture and the motivational inhale before an important exam or public talk, before a sales call, before an important meeting or before an important sports event. Try it even during work. It takes only two minutes of your time, but it can give you energy and motivation for about one hour of efficient work. While writing this book, I got up almost every 45 minutes to perform my MOTIVATIONAL GESTURE, MOTIVATIONAL INHALE AND MOTIVATIONAL SCREAM. The motivation scream? What is that, you ask?

3. THE MOTIVATIONAL SCREAM

The way you use your voice has a big influence on the level of energy in your body and directly affects your motivation. How do you talk when you are thrilled, full of energy, and motivated? Think of sportsmen who are overjoyed with their victories. Which words do they use? YES, SUPER, BRAVO, FANTASTIC, CRAZY. Which motivational words do you use when everything goes smoothly? Why should you use them only then? Use them every day and you will see how you are going to feel. The combination of motivational gestures, motivational inhales and motivational screams is an excellent strategy for overcoming fear, tension, cold feet and even for reducing stress. Go into the woods and scream for a few minutes. Then try to find out where your stress has gone!

> "The secret of the success of every successful man is hidden in the fact that he has developed different habits from those who aren't successful."
>
> A. Jackson King

Do you still not believe that these techniques can influence your well-being and motivation? Has it ever happened that you were at a seminar where you almost fell asleep? How was the speaker talking? Was he speaking slowly, sleepily, without accents, without changing the speed of the talk, without energy in his voice? Did he have very limited body gestures and facial expressions or did he perhaps even sit down? Do not fall asleep! Get up now and do the winning inhale, scream and gesture.

How do you feel now?

Why does this happen? Because it has been proven that our influence on others depends:

- 7% on the words we use.
- 38% on our voice (speed, volume, pace, tone).
- 55% on body language and facial expression.

Consider that the next time you perform in front of a group of people. Because these facts are so important, we teach them in our workshops on skills for public appearances.

4. POSTURE

Posture (how you stand, how you sit, how you walk) greatly affects your well-being and motivation.

EMOTIONAL STRATEGIES FOR MOTIVATION

Do you remember the most boring lesson at school? How were you sitting at the table and on the chair? Try to sit now in that way and pay attention to how you feel. With correct posture, people can change their mood, emotions and level of motivation in no time at all.

What affects your mood and motivation?

The position of the shoulders, the position of the arms, thorax (uplifted or slumped) and the position of the head (upright, down, leaning to the left or to the right) all influence mood and motivation.

EXERCISE 34

Sit on a chair as if you feel like a 5 on a depression scale from 1 to 10. How would you sit? Where would your hands be? How would you hold your legs? Where would your head be turned? How would you breathe? What would be your muscle tone?

Now sit down as if you felt like a 10 on the scale of depression. How are you sitting? Perhaps you are already lying down!

Now, sit down on a chair as if you were wildly self-confident, motivated and determined. Now! How are you sitting? What is your posture now? It is certainly very different!

When did you feel better? Adopt as "yours" that position in which you feel the best. Many people ask me what to do when they are very depressed, angry or nervous. Usually, I answer them, "Can you show me how you do that?" Their reaction is shock. "How do you mean how I do that?" they tell me, "I'm simply depressed."

> "Success is a state of mind. If you want success, start thinking of yourself as a success."
> Dr. Joyce Brothers

Each of us has his or her own strategy or recipe for how to become depressed, sad, angry or nervous. To fall into these moods you have to use the body in a certain way; you have to tell yourself certain things and focus on certain things (let me remind you of the chapter on feelings). Usually, simultaneously with changing the pose of the body, we change our feelings. Why? It is because our body is trained so that we use a specific strategy or recipe for specific emotions. Just as each cook has a personal recipe for apple pie, we each have our own recipe for specific emotions.

Fundamentally, we are responsible for everything we feel. We always have available all the resources with which to change our emotions. Until now, maybe you have not been aware of this fact, but from now on you will pay attention to the pose of your body, to the words that you are speaking to yourself and to the thoughts that are going through your mind. At the seminar for motivation, we learn how to deal with emotions that can give us a life without heavy stress, nervousness and anxiety. These are emotions we create for ourselves. It is worth trying this technique because your life can change forever.

5. FACIAL EXPRESSIONS

EXERCISE 35

Smile as if you have heard the most beautiful thing you can think of. Let your face be decorated with a million-dollar smile. Now, while laughing, try to be first angry, then nervous and last, depressed.

You can't? This exercise has been done by thousands of people at my seminars. They always find that it is almost impossible, or very hard, to do that. Facial expressions dominate our attention. Try to concentrate your thoughts on something negative, but keep a million-dollar smile on your face. It has been proven that your facial expression affects your emotions and thus also your motivation.

Months ago "Nataša", who suffered from anorexia, came to me for personal counseling. When I asked her to describe her feelings, she said that she was nervous all the time. When I told her to show me, she started nervously walking up and down, wrinkling her forehead, chin and her whole face. She kept nervously touching each of her fingers. When I asked her to beautify her face with a million-dollar smile, while staying nervous, she was completely confused. The expression on her face and the movements of her arms and body were not coherent, and in that way we broke her pattern of behavior. Then, we switched the statement "I'm nervous" to "I'm curious" and the feelings were gone in a moment.

6. MUSIC

Music is one of the best aids to increase motivation. Why? Because it allows you to combine all the other listed physical strategies of motivation. What happens when you hear your favorite song? Suddenly, you start to sway to the rhythm of the music, or start singing, which changes the expression on your face, and with words, you change your focus. What happens when you sing, "We are the Champions?"

7. SMELL

Smell can have a very big influence on the level of your motivation. What happens when you smell something unpleasant? What is the expression on your face, what is your posture? What do you say to yourself? It isn't very motivating, is it? More information about how smells affect motivation can be learned in books on aromatherapy.

> "Success is the reward for those who never give up."
> Napoleon Hill

3 MENTAL HABITS OF LONG TERM MOTIVATION

or long-term motivation, you only have to remember the three most important mental habits of motivation. Although there are just a few, they are very important for your well-being and motivation.

1. POSITIVE ATTITUDE

> "A positive attitude is a person's passport to a better tomorrow."
> Anonymous

Actually, the whole book talks about positive attitudes. If you would like to find a chapter on positive attitudes, I suggest you return to the chapter about personal growth. Here, let me repeat: your thoughts depend on you. You are the one who decides what you are going to focus on, and you are the one who decides what significance you will give to events that happen to you. You and nobody else determine how you feel. Your future is in your hands. Now, let us see how your feelings, emotions and, of course, motivation can be affected by the questions which you ask yourself.

2. THE POWER OF QUESTIONS

Do you remember Lidija? Do you recall which questions she was asking herself? No wonder she had suicidal thoughts. Asking the right questions is one of the simplest tools to maintain motivation, a good mood and positive leverage. Besides the questions that we ask ourselves aloud, in our brain, there is a constant process of asking and answering questions. This process goes on subconsciously. Your thoughts will answer any question you ask. Your focus depends on your questions and where you focus your attention determines your emotions; in turn, your emotions determine your actions.

We know the questions, which we ask ourselves from time to time, and we know the (usually) one or at most two questions, which we ask from day to day. We are aware of these questions — consciously or subconsciously. These are called primary questions. The primary questions reflect our values and determine the meaning of our lives. The primary questions are the ones that determine why some people succeed in life while others continue to struggle. Because of the wrong primary questions, people waste their lives.

> "The word which you keep between your lips is your slave, the word spoken out of season is your master."
> - An Arabic proverb

Asking the right questions of yourself, and finding out what causes pain and pleasure in human beings are two important topics at the seminar "The Pyramid of Success." This seminar, where we dedicate as much time as possible to everyone, is the one where many people find the meaning of their lives and set up exciting goals. I call it "Everything is possible." It is true that everything is possible, but only if you have enough motivation, energy, knowledge and somebody to show you the way.

Do you ask yourself the following questions, too?

- Why is this happening to me?
- Why am I such a loser?
- Why can't I lose weight?
- Why can't I stop smoking?
- Why don't other people like me?
- Whom have I wronged that God is taking such revenge on me?

What happens when you ask this kind of question? At the same moment, all your negative experiences, fears, doubts and beliefs go through your mind, and offer you rapid replay.

It is like the idea that what you ask for is what you get. If you do not ask for anything, you cannot get anything. The right questions are also important when you are negotiating with somebody, or you are selling your products. Your questions determine how the person you talk to will decide. For example, ask him how he spent the vacation. If he had a good time, he will start to explain with all his energy the wonderful things he did. Then ask him something negative, something with which he connects negative emotions. Watch what happens to his expression. It will definitely change, because that triggers in his brain certain pictures, which affect the facial expression and body, which then result in a certain range of emotions.

> "Man is what he believes."
> Anton Chekhov

Is it possible to change somebody's emotions within a moment? Of course, we just ask him a question that has nothing to do with the present topic of the conversation. Thus, we cut the line of his thoughts and divert them to another channel. The next time you are in a company where they are going to gossip about somebody, try simply to divert their attention with a question that has nothing to do with the topic of the conversation. Watch what happens!

The right questions are also very important when we solve certain problems, and we seek solutions. Do you remember how I reacted when I came back from the seminar, and colleagues told me the "welcome" news that we had wrongly invested a significant amount of money? I did not ask, "How could you be so incompetent?" The question was what we could learn from the situation, and how we could improve administration, which occupied my mind instead of blame and thus brought positive results for the future of the company. The success of a company also depends on the questions the employees ask themselves.

You have probably noticed that all the negative questions start with "why." If you would like to search for resolution and be more motivated and creative, you have to ask yourself questions which start with "how" and "what":

- How can I succeed?
- How can I lose weight and have fun at the same time?
- What can I do to be better?

The difference in thinking because of positive questions is obvious. From this day forwards, pay attention to the questions that you ask yourself consciously or subconsciously. I can guarantee that your life will change 100%.

> "It does not really matter what we expect from life, but rather what life expects from us."
> Viktor Frankl

3. DAILY MOTIVATIONAL QUESTIONS

I used to suffer from insomnia. When I was studying, I had a roommate who fell asleep within five minutes, while I kept tossing, turning, and asking myself questions:

- Why can't I fall asleep?
- What else do I have to do tomorrow?
- Why can he fall asleep so fast?

Now, I ask myself different questions in the evening and in the morning, ones which give me more energy and pleasure, but most of all the feeling that I am worth something.

- What good deeds have I done today?
- What have I learned today?
- For what can I be thankful today?
- What wonderful things will happen to me tomorrow?
- For whom can I make the day better? Whom do I love?
- Why do I deserve to be happy?
- What have I achieved so that I am proud of myself?

I ask myself these and similar questions in the evening before I fall asleep, in the morning when I wake up and in the office at the break, when I want to motivate myself for further work.

You can ask yourself different questions, but it is important that they make you feel good.

HOW TO DEVELOP YOUR OWN STRATEGY FOR MOTIVATION

Let us use another example: you were at a birthday party for a friend.

You were served excellent cake. You said to yourself, "Hmm, I could bake that kind of cake next week when my friend has a birthday." The birthday arrives and with great enthusiasm, you start making the cake. You are going to try to bake the same one your friend did a week before. What are the chances that you will bake a cake exactly like his? Very unlikely.

> "To be or not to be is not a question of compromise.
> Either you be or you don't be."
>
> Golda Meir

What happens if you get the recipe and exact instructions to make your favorite cake? The first time, perhaps, it will not be so good, but each time it will get better and better. After we get a recipe and we make the cake many times, it gets better.

As with the cake, we need a recipe or strategy to get motivated in a moment, a strategy to overcome fears, a strategy for decisions and for financial independence. In this segment, I offer you "the recipe" for finding a strategy for motivation that you can use repeatedly and instantly achieve a mood of motivation. I suggest that you use it before sales calls, before sales presentations, before meetings, before negotiations, and for improving work efficiency through the day, basically, whenever and wherever you need it. At each moment, you will have access to all your sources of power.

3 BASIC INGREDIENTS IN YOUR RECIPE FOR MOTIVATION

1. VISUAL INGREDIENTS

Some people are more visually oriented; they imagine everything in pictures. You can recognize them because they tend to talk quickly, as if they are commenting on a movie they are watching in their minds. While talking, they constantly use their hands; the head is up and they tell how things and events "look", how they "imagine" things.

EMOTIONAL STRATEGIES FOR MOTIVATION

Pay attention to the following visual elements and verify how the changing of those elements in your mind affects your motivation and mood:

- colors (bright, dark, black, white, colorful);
- the distance from the event you are watching, which puts you in a motivated mood (close, far);
- Where do you see yourself in this picture? (do you watch the event from outside, disassociated, or are you a participant in the picture, associated). When do the stronger feelings emerge?

> **"Better to light one candle than to curse the darkness."**
> Chinese Proverb
>
> **"Better to light one candle than to curse the darkness."**
> Chinese Proverb

2. AUDITORY INGREDIENTS

Some people are more sensitive to the words that they use. They are more motivated by what they hear than by what they see. For them, it is important which words are used to describe something, what the tone is, what the volume of the voice is. "Those oriented toward hearing" will tell you, "Yes, I do HEAR what are you telling me, LISTEN TO..." These differences should be kept in mind with sales, negotiations, persuasions and public talks. I teach those skills in the seminar, "The Pyramid of the Success."

Auditory ingredients that can affect your motivation are:

- Tone of speech.
- Volume of speech.
- Whether it is you who talks or somebody else (some people get motivated by telling themselves, others when they hear somebody else telling them).
- The pace of speech.

EXERCISE 36

Try the following:

Say I LOVE YOU while using the vocal elements you usually use when you are screaming at somebody or angry with somebody. Do this with full emotional intensity. Suddenly, the phrase I LOVE YOU loses sense and meaning. Now do this by saying I HATE YOU in a sexy, gentle, loving voice, and add a seductive look. How different I HATE YOU now sounds, doesn't it?

3. KINESTHETIC INGREDIENTS

The people who are kinesthetic types talk very slowly, in such a way that you can fall asleep. Do you know somebody who talks like that? What do you believe he thinks about you, if you talk fast and loud and use particularly aggressive gestures? You are right if you think he gets scared of you. In order to reach a common goal, you have to adjust to the kind of speech the other person is accustomed to and prefers. Kinesthetic types use words like "heavy," "I feel," and "it occurred to me."

Kinesthetic ingredients that can influence your motivation are:

- Tone of muscles (are they tense or relaxed?); go into a state of motivation and then switch to one of depression and pay attention to the difference in the tension of your muscles.
- What the breathing is like (deep, shallow, fast, slow).
- Whether you feel light or heavy.
- Whether you feel cold or warm.

THE QUESTIONS FOR THE MOTIVATION RECIPE

On vacation in Črna Gora, I met Brankica and her husband. With Helena, we were their guests. One day they invited us with their friends to see some beautiful bays near Budva. Of course, delightedly, we accepted the invitation. Before we went off on the boat, we chatted on the beach a while. When we were to go on board the boat, which we did by walking through knee-deep water, Brankica surprised me with the statement that she was not coming with us because she was afraid of water and boats. Of course, I wanted to know why, because I am so interested in helping others to overcome the various fears, phobias and limiting beliefs that stop them on the way to personal happiness and success. I asked her how long she had been living with the fear and why this happened. I was interested in the strong emotional event that caused that fear in her. She told me that when she was five, she survived a shipwreck. Since then, she had never gone swimming in the sea or been sailing.

> *"He who asks questions cannot avoid the answers."*
> Proverb from Cameroon

That was a challenge for me. I told her that we could solve this problem in 10 minutes. Because she wanted help, I asked her questions that stimulated her sensations of self-confidence, determination and courage. In that way, I helped her find her own strategy for determination, self-confidence, courage and motivation. You can ask these questions to yourself and find what the ingredients are for your personal recipe for motivation.

1. Can you remember a moment when you were very self-confident, motivated and determined?
2. Can you recall the precise moment?
3. Can you concentrate on that moment and relive it again?
4. While remembering this moment, think:

a) What was the first thing that triggered your state of motivation, determination and self-confidence? Was it something you:
- saw?
- heard?
- sensed?

What you picture in your head, what you focus on, is very important. When we want to get into a certain mood, we always concentrate on the same pictures or memories, which then always trigger the same emotions. To get myself into a state of motivation, I simply picture myself standing in front of a crowd of people; I picture their happy faces when they are motivated. I can see a bright moving picture, and I imagine everything in colors.

b) In this way, you then see (hear or sense) a similar situation in your life. What was the next thing that happened to you while in this state? Did you:

EMOTIONAL STRATEGIES FOR MOTIVATION

- Imagine something in your mind?
- Say something to yourself?
- Sense anything?

c) When we have completed parts a and b of the exercise (repeat what you answered or what somebody told you), we ask again:

Did you:

- Imagine something in your mind?
- Say something to yourself?
- Feel any important emotion?

When Brankica answered these questions, I quickly discovered her strategy for motivation. Then, using the technique of anchoring (Richard Bandler technique of Neuro-linguistic programming), I anchored these strategies in her mind. Do you want to know the result? After 10 minutes, Brankica proudly stepped onto a boat for the first time in 23 years and then, with a smile on her face and with clenched fists enjoyed a sail on the sea. With clenched fists! Exactly. Let me explain why. Are you ready to learn one of the techniques that can change your life forever?

ANCHORING, OR SUCCESS LEAVES ITS MARK

Anchoring is the way to make a certain experience permanent. With anchoring, you can create a permanent trigger mechanism that will automatically cause certain positive conditions, which you need to motivate yourself, without having to dwell on it consciously.

All the anchors are associations, thoughts, ideas, sensations or conditions, which are connected with a certain impulse.

The anchors are the associations between a specific impulse and a specific condition. We are not born with these; we create them.

The anchor can be:

- A word.
- A phrase.
- Something we can see, hear, feel, taste or smell.

An example: you see a man (or more than one), and you can switch in a moment into a certain condition, good or bad, that depends on what emotions you connect with him (her or them).

Dr. Ivan Pavlov did an experiment with a group of hungry dogs, in which he presented meat, but they could only see and smell the meat. As soon as they smelled it, they started to salivate. At that point, he rang a bell. Soon, the dogs did not need meat any more to start to salivate. The bell was enough. Pavlov created a very strong neurological connection between ringing the bell and the sensation of hunger and salivation.

Under stress, many people subconsciously run for cigarettes, alcohol, overeating or start to pull out their hair. The impulsive reaction, such as drinking alcohol, becomes a regular way for the person to control the stress.

The goal here is that this procedure now becomes conscious, and that we exchange negative anchors for positive ones, for those that give us power.

What emotions do you experience and what pictures do you see when you remember the following?

- your first day at school
- the hardest examination or subject at school
- a wedding
- the day you graduated
- you see the flag of your country
- the slogan "Just do it"
- the slogan "The impossible is possible"
- the slogan "With motivation to success!"

As you experienced, saw or felt these words, they triggered in your mind certain pictures, and these then triggered certain emotions.

Thus, it can happen that when you hear a certain song, you are instantly in a good mood, and you say to yourself, "Oh, those were the good old days!" The song probably reminds you of some event from the past, such as a first love, a wedding, or a party.

Did you ever pass a person wearing a certain perfume, and you suddenly remembered an old flame? All of these are anchors we have created subconsciously. These very strong associations are well known to advertising companies.

Anchoring can be very important if you want to develop long-lasting, passionate and loving relationships.

Imagine how it would affect your life if you could consciously create conditions under which you are very effective. The best figures in politics, sports, art and the business world have to be capable of having all their sources of power available at any moment.

Likewise, it is also very important that you are able to "turn off." Many businessmen become very motivated; they achieve wonderful results, but they burn out; they are unhappy; they lose their family life or, in extreme examples, get ill (i.e., heart disease and other ailments).

Participants in the seminar for motivation, with the help of techniques of anchoring, summon all the positive emotions of laughter, joy, playfulness, self-confidence, motivation and love, which then help them to achieve top results every day in their personal and professional lives.

Sometimes, because of the incredible power of this exercise at the seminar, somebody cries out of happiness, because he (she) had not experienced so many positive feelings for a very long time. This is also proof that they are able to live every day the life they want and deserve. They find out that the quality of their lives has nothing to do with reality; it depends on the emotions in which they live, and consequently, on what significance they give to certain things.

CREATING A MOTIVATIONAL ANCHOR

When a person is in a very intense emotional state (positive or negative, joy, motivation, depression), at the peak of that state, we add some specific impulse (word, move, gesture, touch). In this way, the specific impulse (specific look, gesture touch or voice) and the specific state are connected. As a result, whenever we trigger this impulse, that state automatically follows.

THE PROCEDURE FOR CREATING A MOTIVATIONAL ANCHOR

Locate precisely the state, feeling or emotion that you would like to anchor (motivation, determination, courage, concentration).

Remember events from your past when you experienced those feelings or that state.

With your mind and body, put yourself back in time and relive those feelings. For this, you have to use your whole body; you must be completely submerged in that emotional state (stand as you were standing then; tense your muscles as they were tensed then; breathe as you breathed then). Increase the intensity of all these feelings.

When you are at the peak of the emotional state that you would like to anchor, you have to add a specific physical trigger (a gesture of victory, a clenched fist, even a word) and repeat all of this with total emotional intensity at least 6 times.

Then, return to a normal state. Now, suddenly trigger all the anchors (gesture, word, clenched fist). If you have done the procedure in the correct order and with total emotional intensity, you should feel the energy in your body immediately. This technique can be used every day. The more often you use it, the more effective it will be.

Professional sportsmen can also use the technique of anchoring. I taught this technique to our women's ski team, after being invited by their long-time coach, Pavel Goršič. They were thrilled with the effectiveness of the techniques. Try them yourself - you won't be sorry!

ANCHOR FOR COURAGE

I remember a girl at the motivational seminar. She was so shy that she became frightened of a man if he so much as looked at her, not to mention if he approached her. Her whole body shrank in fear, and she started to cry. In order to help her, I had to approach her very carefully. I saw within a minute what the problem was. First, I anchored feelings of self-confidence and courage in her with the procedure described; and then I added, besides the anchors she chose for herself, an anchor with a touch on her left shoulder. Afterwards, I invited a man to attack her, literally. At the same moment that he was attacking her, I triggered on her left shoulder the positive anchor of courage and self-confidence. Instead of being afraid, as she would have been before, because of the newly created anchor, she stood up to him. The participants were very surprised at how strong the technique of anchoring can be.

This technique can be also used by sales clerks who are afraid of calling customers by phone or fearful of sales presentations.

> *"Progress and development are impossible if we react every time in the same way we have always done."*
>
> - Wayne Dyer

EMOTIONAL STRATEGIES FOR MOTIVATION

I hope that by now you are convinced of the importance and strength of the techniques of motivation. Moreover, I hope that you will use these in your everyday life because they do have an amazing effect. Do you remember the chapter in which I talked about improving life by only 0.5% daily? Do not expect that you will master everything the very first day, because you did not learn to walk in the first month of your life. Just as a seed of wheat needs some time to sprout, so too you will be more ready each day for success, by applying daily the knowledge and techniques from this book.

> "You cannot discover new seas if you are afraid of losing the coast from your sight."
> - Anonymous

That is why I am moving on to reveal the last secret of motivAction...

SECRET #7:

THE TREASURER OF MOTIVATION

MONEY AND CAREER

"How much wealth we have depends on what we do with it. If we use it wisely, we will have just enough, if we use it unwisely, we are going to be always short of it."

Christian Bovee

"Experience shows that success is due less to ability than to zeal. The winner is he who gives himself to that work body and soul."

Charles Buxton

IN THIS CHAPTER, YOU WILL FIND OUT ABOUT:

How to regain control over your life instead of letting life control you.

ಆ

How finally to take your financial destiny into your hands.

ಆ

How, with the help of 6 steps, to reach TOTAL FINANCIAL FREEDOM, so that you won't need to work for money again.

ಆ

The 9 most common financial fears which block us on the way to financial freedom.

ಆ

How to double your income and have more spare time.

ಆ

How to increase your income quickly.

CAREER AND MONEY

I hope that you have not skipped the previous chapters and started to read right here. It would not be wrong, because the book is written so that you can start to read anywhere. However, if you have read all the previous chapters, especially the chapter about emotions and goals, then you should know already which work would bring you the most pleasure – the work that would be your dream career. In this chapter, I will touch on some basic emotional burdens and limiting beliefs that stop us from becoming financially independent. Do you want to become financially independent? What is financial independence anyway? And how can you increase your income by 30% in one year? Are you interested?

YOUR BELIEFS ABOUT MONEY AND WEALTH

Our beliefs about money are usually deeply rooted within us. Many give me cross looks if I ask them: "How much money would you like to earn?"

Please SINCERELY answer this question:

Would you like to be wealthy?

At my seminars, I also ask: "Who here would like to be rich?" There are only a few who dare to lift up their hands and say firmly, "I would like to be rich!" The most common answers are, "Who wouldn't like to be? Well, not too rich; wealthy enough to live comfortably; to be rich enough that so it wouldn't spoil me; moderately wealthy; I would rather not be rich because money spoils people; I would rather be wealthy in other senses." After that, I usually joke around, "With the word wealthy I didn't mean only money; to be wealthy can also mean something else!" And everybody is relieved.

This reaction happens because many people connect wealth with negative emotions. These negative emotions arise because of limiting beliefs that people have about money. If you are one of those who would really like to be rich, I would like to know how much that would mean monthly? The majority of people do not have clear financial goals. Money means something negative to them and something they have to work hard for.

A very successful businesswoman, Irena hired me not long ago for personal counseling. She had run her business for years. She hired me mostly because she believed that she earned less than she was worth. She asked me what I thought her problem was, because she was convinced that she did not know how to earn money. Before we even met, I told her that most likely the problems laid in her attitudes toward money and the beliefs she had about money and work. I found out that she really had a high motivation to earn more money, but deep within herself, she believed that she did not deserve it. The problem was only in her limiting beliefs connected with money. One of the reasons that you began to read this book must also be that you would like to have more freedom, more independence and more security. In addition, I am sure that goes for emotional and financial independence.

> "Money represents a pile of things without value or a pile of things without use, but it also represents something precious, and that is independence!"
> - Samuel Smiles

Until you analyze the beliefs you have about money, you certainly will not taste your desired financial freedom. You will find out that your reason tells you something else about money than your emotions. It is like two horses in harness pulling each to its own side.

I found out that people have two main beliefs about money that stop them from being financially independent:

- they do not believe that they deserve to have more money
- they believe that they are successful only if they have a lot of money.

MONEY ITSELF DOESN'T BRING HAPPINESS AND PLEASURE

Peter is a very successful businessman. He is in the life-insurance business. He believed for a long time that money is the real and the only symbol of success. He is of the belief that without money he wouldn't be successful. Peter is a nice guy; whoever meets him has to like him; he is very energetic, full of laughter, likes to joke and is very kind to everybody. Each year he competes with himself to earn more money than the year before. He asked me if I could help him with some advice. He was under stress because of too much work all the time. And although he had more businesses, five cars and expensive clothes, he was not satisfied.

> "Happiness comes with spiritual and not with financial wealth."
> John M. Templeton

At one counseling session, I asked him what thrilled him about his work. The answer? The money. At the end, he admitted that he did not really enjoy his work, no matter how many hours he worked, but the kind of money he earned there, he could not have earned anywhere else.

When I asked him what would happen if he drove a less fancy car, and he had a more modest office, he answered that this would mean failure to him. In his opinion, money is a measure of success.

So what was Peter was doing wrong? He was connecting happiness and pleasure with money. He thought that money was the key to satisfaction and fulfillment. Money was also a tool that allowed him to feel important. I am of the belief that each of us can have as much money he wishes and live the life that makes him happy. That is what I talk about in this book and at the seminars I give. Life is not and should not be one big sacrifice for a big pile of money. At the end of your life, you probably are not going to remember how much money you earned. You will remember the most wonderful moments you lived through. Subsequently, Peter decided to entrust the management of his company to his business partner. For himself, he decided to find happiness in other things; he found peace, happiness and contentment.

Does that mean that you have to be poor? Of course not. That means that you should stop running after money in order to feel important. Just pay attention to the wheel of life so that it will run through your life smoothly. Only in that way will you have all the happiness, contentment and wealth you deserve.

MONEY AND CAREER

EXERCISE 37

WHAT DOES MONEY MEAN TO YOU?

Without thinking, finish the following sentences. Write down anything that comes to mind.

Rich people are..._____

Money is only..._____

Because of money people do..._____

My parents told me that money is..._____

Money is..._____

My friends think that money is..._____

If I were rich, I wouldn't... _____

I think that money is..._____

To be crazy rich is like.._____

Money... _____

Money creates... _____

The word rich reminds me of.. _____

The word poor reminds me of.. _____

CHANGE YOUR BELIEFS ABOUT MONEY AND GET RICH

An old belief	A new belief
I'm not smart enough to be rich.	I have to educate myself constantly and work smart.
I will never be rich.	I am already rich, I just have to use my capabilities.
I have to sacrifice and work hard.	Money is only the logical consequence of constant progression.
Money spoils people.	With money, I could help people.

YOU DON'T NEED TO EARN MILLIONS IN ORDER TO BECOME A MILLIONAIRE

Many people think that they can become rich from what they earn. Many pursue money daily, but they forget that the formula for wealth is very simple: spend less than you earn, and invest the difference. The profit that is created from investments, use only partially, invest the rest again. Most people live the opposite way. Everything they have they spend, and they also borrow money. They take out high-interest payday loans to cover expenses, without even thinking that they will have to pay it back next month.

> "The borrower is servant to the lender."
> The Book of Proverbs 22:7

MONEY AND CAREER

During financial counseling, I often come across the fact that people are afraid to invest money. When I started to sell life insurance, there were few people who trusted this form of savings and insurance. Today almost everybody is aware that for basic social security and some additional pension they need to have life and accident insurance. In between there appear some other forms of savings. For example, saving in funds, about which you can read in more detail in the international bestseller, From the Journal of a Millionaire or The Wealth is Within Us by Boris Vene and Nikola Grubiša. In the meantime, they have also founded the so-called pension funds. People are confused because they have just found out and started to trust their savings to insurance companies, and now here is a new form of savings. They are afraid of investing money, because they are afraid of losing it. They are afraid because they do not have enough knowledge.

In order for you to become a millionaire, you have to know some basics about how to treat money.

Just some more basic advice on how to gain financial independence: if you put aside from the age of 25 approximately $1,000 at 10% yearly interests, you would be a millionaire 65 times over. You don't believe it?

Remember the chapter about increasing your efficiency by only 0.5% daily. Remember: you are not going to get rich from what you earn; you will get rich from what you save.

PAY YOURSELF FIRST AND START RIGHT AWAY

The majorities of us like to use an excuse that the right time for saving has not yet come. The most common excuses I hear are:

"I bought a new car and I don't have money; now I'm building a house; I'm going on vacation; after the new year; when I earn some more; there is one investment ahead of me; I'm too old and it won't pay off; when the children are grown up; now school starts..." The list of excuses goes on and on.

Time is passing; the money is not coming from anywhere. To whom would you rather be giving money? To the one who worked hard the whole week, or to the one who didn't deserve it? Don't you think it is fair that you deserve to keep some money if you worked for it for 42 hours or more weekly?

As soon as you earn it, invest 10% of it. Investments are not line loans or shopping. This is money that will go for your future, for the time when you do not need to work, at least not for money. It is about your pension. Do not ever touch this money. Nothing so important can happen. Actually, you have to pay the country more than 10%! Who deserves the money more, the government or you? I recommend the book, The Richest Man in Babylon (George S. Clason) to learn about that as well. This book contains a lot of good advice from ancient times. Why should we invent something new when you can follow the wise advice of ancient philosophers?

> "It is the way of a wise man to keep himself today for tomorrow, and not to venture all his eggs in one basket."
> - Miguel de Cervantes

I have often heard that it is necessary to put 10% of your income towards charity. I did not believe how this can confirm for you that you have enough for your own survival. When I donated for the first time to those in need, I was overwhelmed with a sensation of joy and love. To help somebody who really needs help is the highest form of contribution. When you give, you also get. Do you remember the law of what you sow, you reap?

> "To contribute to charity brings prosperity and honour."
>
> John M. Templeton

6 STEPS TO ABSOLUTE FINANCIAL FREEDOM

The ideas described in the 6 steps to absolute financial freedom occurred to me after years of working in the field with clients, where I saw the kinds of financial problems people were encountering. I found out that we do not know how to set financial goals; we do not know what we should be doing in order to get rid of financial stress, which is very threatening in today's society. When you follow the listed instructions, then you will get the feeling that you hold your financial destiny in your hands. You will feel self-confident and safe because you will know where to direct your ship of success. Each of us has the right to realize our financial goals. In order for dreams to come true, you have to know exactly what these goals are. If you consider the following steps, you will find out exactly what you have to do for your security and for the security of your family and which financial dreams you most want to fulfill.

1. FINANCIAL PROTECTION

This is the first and the least financial goal which each of you should achieve. The purpose of financial protection is that you can be sure that you and your family are financially well taken care of, no matter what happens to you in your life. Financial protection for yourself and your family will be realized after taking care of the next goals:

a) Always have enough liquid property so that you can cover living costs for at least 2 -24 months, that depends on your personal goals. This is money that it is best to keep in the bank in case you lose your job, and you can overcome financial problems until you find a new one. That is the first goal you have to achieve.

b) Make a contract for life insurance that ensures:

- if something tragic happens to you, your family will be taken care of. A recommended insurance sum is one that will cover the cost of living for your family for at least three years after the possible tragic event.

- you must be able, from the insurance sum (the amount which is predicted at the end of the insurance) to pay off all your loans and debts.

c) With other sources (rent, interest) you can get sufficient income for you to continue with the same lifestyle as you were accustomed to before something tragic happened to you.

d) Take out accident insurance with a sum that would allow you, despite disability, to continue with the lifestyle to which you had been accustomed. Private businessmen (your income depends strictly on your personal work) also have to take care of daily compensation, in case they are incapable of working for a long period.

2. FINANCIAL SECURITY

Financial security will be achieved when you have, with the help of different investments, created so much capital that, at minimal 8% interest (you can be sure of that with investments in mutual funds) you can provide yourself enough money so that you could, even if you could not work, satisfy the following needs:

a) make the monthly payment on the loan for your apartment (until it is paid off). If you are paying rent, then the amount for rent.

b) provide enough money for your and your family's needs monthly.

c) ensure payment of all the costs of the apartment (electricity, garbage disposal, gas, heating and water).

d) pay the costs of the car (registration, road taxes, regular services, insurance and service check, fuel)
e) keep all the insurance (life, accident and health).
f) pay taxes to the government.

> "A good reputation is more valuable than money."
> - Publilius Syrus

3 FINANCIAL CONFIDENCE

You will achieve financial freedom with the help of different investments that create so much capital it would, at minimal 8% interest (you can be guaranteed that with investments in mutual funds) provide enough money so you could always cover the costs of financial security and of the next four financial goals, even if you never worked again:

a) that you can in total or partially help your children to cover the costs of their education, which is very important.
b) that you can still save in different forms (insurance, banks, funds, shares, real estate) which will allow you an even better financial future;
c) that you can satisfy your needs for enjoyment, entertainment (vacation, theatre, restaurants) in the amount of 50% of what you are enjoying now;
d) that you can still afford new clothes and shoes.

4. FINANCIAL INDEPENDENCE

You will achieve financial independence when, with the help of different investments, you create enough capital it can, at minimum interest of 8% (you can be guaranteed that with investments in mutual funds), ensure you sufficient money so you can always enjoy the standard YOU HAVE TODAY (consider inflation), although you never work again.

In addition, a question: Would you quit your job if you could have enough money to assure you the same standard of living you have now?

5. FINANCIAL FREEDOM

You will achieve financial freedom when you, with the help of different investments, create the capital which would, at minimal 8% interest (you can be guaranteed that with investments in mutual funds) be sure of sufficient money that you could always live by the standards YOU WANT (consider inflation), even if you never worked again.

6. ABSOLUTE FINANCIAL FREEDOM

You will achieve absolute financial freedom when you, with the help of different investments, create the capital which will bring you, at minimal 8% interest (you can be guaranteed that with investments in mutual funds) enough money so you could do always what you want, whatever you want, wherever you want with whomever you want, and, of course, in a way that will help you and others.

I suggest that you calculate precisely your monthly costs and then make a plan to achieve all six steps to absolute financial freedom. For assistance, you can also turn to our experts who would be delighted to cure you of:

9 THE MOST COMMON FEARS CONNECTED WITH MONEY

Working in financial counseling, I have seen that people have similar fears connected with money. Because of these, they undergo stress, which is reflected in overreaction anxiety, depression, insomnia, nervousness, aggression, diminished sex drive, alcohol abuse, smoking abuse or neglect of children and of the family.

> "The fear of saving and losing money stops us from creating a rich life"
> - Smiljan Mori

1. THE FEAR OF LOSS OF TODAY'S JOB

Many people are afraid of losing their present job. They are afraid of change, new challenges. The only cure for that is to use the techniques for overcoming fear and anxiety described in this book. I also suggest you simultaneously develop other skills and capabilities to give you the feeling that you are each day more important to your company, or find yourself an additional part-time job.

2. THE FEAR OF BEING INCAPABLE OF EARNING MONEY FOR FOOD, CLOTHES AND OTHER BASIC NEEDS OF THE FAMILY.

3. THE FEAR THAT YOU WON'T BE ABLE TO SUPPORT THE EDUCATION OF YOUR CHILDREN

The only solution is that you start to think today about the fact that your child will need money for study and further education. At least, you will have to help him in the beginning.

4. THE FEAR OF LOSING ALL THE MONEY AND WEALTH YOU HAVE EARNED

Human beings are very weird creatures. Working with successful businessmen, I discovered something big. Most of them were living at the beginning in fear of not earning enough money. When they earned even more than they anticipated, they become afraid of losing it. In this way, we run in circles around different fears and beliefs.

5. THE FEAR OF HAVING TOO MANY LOANS

That fear blocks many people to such an extent that they do not dare to be engaged with their own business and invest, which might bring them big profits.

That fear is healthy in a way, because it forces us to use money wisely. But we can also meet people who do not have that fear at all. They keep borrowing money all over, and they do not even think how to pay it back.

6. THE FEAR OF LOSING THEIR HOME IF THEY GET DIVORCED

That is not so surprising, knowing that every third marriage ends in divorce. Many insist on the "status quo," which causes physic pain to themselves, and to their partner and children - just because of that fear.

7. THE FEAR OF LOSING THEIR REPUTATION IN SOCIETY IF THEY LOSE MONEY

Many people use money to appear important in front of others. In their wish to be appreciated, they overspend, and that can bring them to bankruptcy. Handle money carefully. By itself, money does not bring a good self-image, nor will it solve other problems.

> "The gratification of wealth is not found in mere possession, as in lavish expenditure, but in its wise application."
>
> Miguel de Cervantes

8. THE FEAR OF NOT HAVING ENOUGH MONEY WHEN THEY RETIRE

This is what this book talks about. How to get rid of fears, limiting beliefs, unnecessary worries, how to motivate yourself for the top achievements, that we could one day be healthy and happy in the last third of our life.

9. THE FEAR OF LOSING INVESTED MONEY

Many games of luck have been popular in our country. They promised big earnings without big effort and high interest, which most of the time was never paid out. We have to distinguish between games of luck and investments in legal savings forms that are well known all over the world. Instead of being stopped by fear on the way to financial independence, arm yourself with the knowledge that will give you a sense of security. Only in that way can you become a treasurer of your financial independence.

THE THREE BUCKETS - WHICH IS THE FULLEST.

There are many who don't save because of different fears, and there are some who invest wrongly. Some keep their savings at home, for which they get no interest. Others mostly trust their savings to banks, where they get the lowest interest; one third invest all their savings in the stock market, which can bring the biggest profits, but is also the riskiest. If you would like to reach financial freedom in a safe way, I suggest that you divide your savings into "three buckets" and definitely consult with an expert because the way you invest very much depends on your age, your years to retirement, goals and the capital which is available to you.

Imagine your savings on the way to financial independence like three buckets.

THE DIAMOND BUCKET

This one has to be the safest of all. Here you keep the money that you will need for your 2 to 24 months reserve, money for the education of your children, for the cost of your apartment.

In this bucket are safe investments in life insurance, in state bonds, in mutual funds, in savings at the bank.

THE GOLDEN BUCKET

In this bucket are investments, which help you to create bigger profits. These kinds of investments are not as safe as those in the diamond bucket. They do not give you guarantees but they are, in the long-term, safe and reasonable investments. Despite that, you have to take the risk yourself. These are investments in mutual funds, mixed or shareholder funds, and investments in share holds. You should never put all of your money in this bucket, because the capital market is very unpredictable; you first have to achieve financial protection, financial security and so forth.

THE RULE: All the profits from the GOLDEN BUCKET you must then share between the three buckets again.

1/3 of the profit from the GOLDEN BUCKET goes back into the DIAMOND BUCKET, because in that way, you confirm the foundations of your financial independence.

1/3 of the profit you can reinvest in the GOLDEN BUCKET.

1/3 of the profit you can "invest" in a DREAM BUCKET or A BOTTOMLESS BUCKET.

THE DREAM BUCKET OR THE BOTTOMLESS BUCKET

This bucket is the fullest for the majority. In this bucket are things we do like to afford: new clothes, cars, travel, jewelry, house furniture, various fashionable accessories. In this bucket, we can put only so much of our income as is left over from the

DIAMOND and THE GOLDEN BUCKET. Most people often stuff their DREAM BUCKET before the month is over, so they barely get to the next salary. And here lies the reason why so many people die bankrupt. If you are always going to start to save after you have filled THE BOTTOMLESS BUCKET, you will keep saying to yourself that you will start saving when you have more money.

> "The real duty of man isn't to show off power and pile up wealth beyond his needs, but to enjoy and enrich his most valuable possession - his soul."
>
> - Gilbert Highet

THE INSURANCE WE ALL NEED BUT OFTEN FORGET

Most of us buy various types of insurance like car or property insurance. We keep forgetting insurance of the most valuable assets we have, insurance of ourselves. Many times we remember this when it is too late. All the manuals which talk about the basics of financial planning warn us that we have to take care of our own security and the security of our loved ones, for example, if something unpredictable happens (accident, disability or death). I am not going to write about what you should do for your financial security, because that is the topic of one of our seminars on how to manage the money. I would like you to start at least thinking about it before it is too late. Somehow, I cannot get the following proverb out of my head:

> "To start to save money when you need it or make a contract for insurance when it is too late is like starting to dig a well when you are already thirsty."
>
> Roman Toplak

HOW MUCH INSURANCE DO YOU NEED IN ALL?

When you are going to make a contract for life insurance, you must be careful that your insurance sum (that is the sum you will get at the end of the insurance term for which the contract was made) will cover all the needs for the family if something tragic happens to you. If you live with a partner, or don't have children, you have to ask if your partner would be able to continue to live with the same standard. You also have to pay attention to outstanding loans. If you have children, you have to provide life insurance for each child's needs to the age of maturity, just in case something happens to both parents. So, how to determine the correct insurance sum? If you decide to have counseling from insurance agents, they will surely know how to recommend to you the correct insurance sum, of course if you trust them with your financial details. One of the simplest ways to determine the amount of insurance for yourself is to multiply your yearly incomes by the number of years until the child reaches 18. For example, if you and your partner together earn $13,000 yearly (net) and you have two children aged 8 and 10. The amount of insurance can be calculated like this:

THE INSURANCE SUM =(common incomes) x (years till age 18/ number of children)

   =($13,000)x(10+8)/2

   =($13,000)x9

   =$117,000

Each of the partners should have insurance to the amount of $58,500 if both have the same salaries, otherwise the amount of yearly payments should be divided proportionately in relation to their salaries. We assume that both have the same salary. However, the insurance sum should always cover all the costs of the expenses, which arrive, with the loss of one of the partners. If you are not able to pay monthly as much as you should, we suggest that you aim at least for an insurance sum to cover living costs for the next three year after a tragic event. As long as the family should need to recover from the loss of their beloved and the financial source. of the partners should have insurance to the amount of $58,500 if both have the same salaries, otherwise the amount of yearly payment should be divided proportionately in relation to their salaries. We assume that both have the same salary. However, the insurance sum should always cover all the costs of the expenses, which arrive, with the loss of one of the partners. If you are not able to pay monthly as much as you should, we suggest that you aim at least for an insurance sum to cover living costs for the next three year after a tragic event. As long as the family should need to recover from the loss of their beloved and the financial source.

START TO SAVE FOR THE CHILDRENS' EDUCATION

Many children would study at university if their parents had enough money to finance their studies in a distant city. The University degree will soon be a ticket to the labor market. Start saving now so that you will not blame yourself for not having taken proper care of your child's education. To find out easily how much money your child would need to study, I suggest you ask parents who have children at university already. They are the best to ask how much they need monthly for their students. When you calculate how much money you should save, you should consider inflation as well. The children will be very grateful. Some money you will contribute; some they will earn for themselves if they follow the advice for students and pupils number 3.

EIGHT HOURS DAILY IS BARELY ENOUGH TO SURVIVE

If you are working eight hours daily, that is barely enough to cover the basic life needs. If you want to become financially independent and afford a little bit more than the majority, or to take care of the education of your children, you will have to add to these eight hours at least two more hours daily. I know that this is not easy along with all the commitments you have at work, at home and maybe somewhere else. Even I used to work only until three p.m. When I exchanged 120 thousand (tolars) of police salary overnight for 70 thousand of the beginning salary at the court, and moreover, increased my living costs from 16.000 to 60.000 monthly, the instinct for survival was triggered in me. When I quit the old job, I was not thinking about that. Then I had to earn an additional 100.000 monthly in order to survive. In a second, I was pushed out of the comfort zone, and I started to take part-time jobs to survive. Of course, it was not easy; it ruined my blood pressure and since then I do not live the same life. But a hard life is not enough to becoming wealthy; you have to use your head too.

SKI-JUMP FOR WINNERS

Sometimes a person has to fall a little, so he can then jump even higher. Some like to use the expression for that, "I'm totally at the bottom." I do like to reply: "Maybe you went there just to take a run." I encourage you to take a run, which will allow you to jump further into a nicer future. Just think of the jumpers, whose jumps also depend, among other things, on the height, from which they take the run. The bigger the run, the further they will jump. But height doesn't make much sense without the technique of gliding on the ski jump, the right timing to push off and the techniques of flying through the air. You have learnt up to now all the techniques and skills that jumpers should master. And now you just have to take the run that will help you fly into a better future. Another warning: even the jumpers did not take off from the highest point the very first day. Gradually go higher and higher every day and be aware that only at the top of the run will you see where you are jumping to. Until then, you have to trust yourself and believe in anything you can achieve.

> "Wealth is the product of man's capacity to think."
>
> - Ayn Rand

HOW TO EARN MORE

If you run a private business, this chapter is going to be very interesting to you--although the advice is also useful for those who are employed in companies, because it can be of some use there as well.

DOUBLE YOURSELF

Doubling yourself does not mean the same as to delegate. To delegate means to find somebody who replaces you in work that you perform well with somebody who will perform it instead of you. You probably know the statement, "Yes, but it isn't so easy to find somebody who can replace me, and work as well as me." That does not mean that you have to find your copy. That means that you have to find somebody who can perform a certain task instead of you. For example: if you would like to double your sales, you have to find somebody who is as good at sales as you are. It is very important that you leave your ego "a little bit to the side" if you want this kind of duplication. In my company, I give the opportunity to the best colleagues to replace me in tasks that I used to perform myself. In this way, Marjan, Kristijan, Toni, Roman, Brane, Jože, Alen and Marjan replace me in those jobs for which I used to believe that I was the only one. When you give people an opportunity to prove themselves, they pay you back with great enthusiasm and they can take a big load off your shoulders. In this way, you can be more productive in the areas where you are really the best.

ADD MORE VALUE TO YOUR CUSTOMERS

The amount you are earning right now is only a reflection of how much value you are giving to your clients right now. This means: if you want to earn more money, you have to become more valuable to clients. Think how you could improve the products or services you offer. Or could you be better in your field? How? When you are the best in your field people want to work with you. To find out easily how to give more value to your clients, put yourself into their shoes. Do you want satisfied and loyal customers?

> "Build a better mousetrap and the world will beat a path to your door."
> Ralph Waldo Emerson

Ask yourself the following questions:

1. What are my clients paying me for?
2. What do my clients need, that the competition, or we don't offer them?
3. What do my clients wish that I don't offer?
4. With which problems do clients most often meet, and could it mean a business opportunity for me?

Call your clients and ask them these questions. You will be surprised at what ideas you will get based on their answers.

MONEY AND CAREER

HANDLE YOUR TIME WISELY

Each of us has 24 hours a day. Despite that, many people still say that they do not have enough time for many things. Whenever I hear this excuse I like to joke, "If you want more time I suggest that you get up an hour earlier every day." Usually they laugh and agree to that idea. Since we all have the same hours available each day, it is true that it depends on everyone what is done with it. That depends on what goals we have in our life, and on whether we know how to set priorities and focus on important things.

> "Lost time is never found."
> - Benjamin Franklin

For more than a year, I was saying that I would write a book. I was writing, but only in my head. I was gaining the experience, connecting events and making an approximate plan for the book. I kept telling myself that I still did not have time, because I had to do so many things first. I was doing them, but they were not of such importance. One day in our company, the idea emerged to market our product through the TV. The idea aroused in me such motivation that I wrote a book within a week. Even I cannot believe that I managed to do that. I was just writing as if I were in a trance. After I left the office, I could still see the computer screen and my fingers pounding the keyboard. I was writing day and night and slept for only five hours daily. Besides that, I had at this time two job interviews, I went to fitness 4 times, on three days for three hours I worked with children from the Youth Centre of Maribor whom we invited to active holidays; I learned so much working with them that I could write another book. After all that, I would like to tell you that you can always find enough time for everything if you have a clear goal and a deadline by which you would like to achieve that goal. I have read many books about how handle the time in order to be more productive. I collected this advice and offer it in the seminar The Perfect Life.

I am of the belief that a man who has clear goals, the necessary motivation and an exact plan can achieve more in one year than others in ten years or even in a lifetime.

SHORT ADVICE THAT CAN DOUBLE YOUR PRODUCTIVITY, YOUR INCOME AND YOUR SPARE TIME

EXERCISE 37

After the following criteria, write down three of the most important tasks you perform at work. Tasks which:

- bring you the most money
- offer you the most pleasure
- are important for company development
- demand your responsibility

MONEY AND CAREER

1._____

2._____

3._____

After you write down the tasks, tell yourself that you will dedicate 80% of your time to them (Pareto principle—it is named for the Italian economist Pareto). Dedicate the remaining 20% to not so important tasks. This method alone, can double your efficiency in less than three months.

1. Each day make a list of priority tasks. Check carefully whether these tasks belong among the three most important tasks on your daily list of tasks. If they are not, consciously put them there. If you cannot do that, despite the abundance of work you have through the day, you will go to bed dissatisfied. You get that feeling if you are not performing the tasks, which are important to you. Remember it does not even matter how much you work. What is important is how wisely you work.

2. For at least a week, write down every 15 minutes the jobs and tasks, which you perform during a typical workweek. With this kind of note taking, you will find out which tasks you do, when you usually do them and how much time they take. In this way, you will be able to combine different tasks in some areas of your responsibilities and do them in a one-time block instead of jumping from one task to the other. With this kind of note, taking you will avoid a sense of no productivity and constant work. In our company, we avoid hiring new people because of the continuous recording and analyzing of jobs and tasks. Productivity increased by 100%.

3. At the end of the week analyze the results from the previous week and, based on your projects and unfinished tasks, plan the daily work for the next week. (I make my plan on Sunday evening when I have the most peace).

4. When you are going to plan tasks and jobs, think about the results you would like to achieve in the next working week. Results are not the same as activity. If you focus on results, you might drop some activities because, for your success, the final result is important, and not the activities. You can be very active, but the results of your work are not visible. It does not matter if some results of the work are visible later, let your thoughts and focus always be on the final result.

> **"Activity isn't the same as the result."**
> Smiljan Mori

5. Don't be disturbed by occasional visitors. If you have work, which demands many contacts with people, it is best that you plan all meetings for one day. I suggest that you organize work in the following pattern (of course it depends on your work):
a) administration (the end of the week)
b) communication with coworkers (the beginning of the week)
c) communication with key clients
d) creating, planning

Over the next week do the task from advice # 2, because in that way you will more easily define your areas of work.

6. When you start a certain task, stay with it until you finish it. If you jump from one task to the other, you are losing concentration and productivity as well.

> "Nobody who doesn't waste time will complain that he has a shortage of it."
> - Thomas Jefferson

7. Take time to exercise, even though you have got plenty to do, because that will increase your productivity by more than 100%. In the beginning, of course, it is not going to be like that, because you will be tired afterward, but later, because of physical activity, you are going to be able to produce much more.

THE CONCLUSION

I congratulate you; you have reached the end of the book. There are few people who read it to the end, and even fewer who use everything they read in their practice, at their work and in their personal lives. And even fewer are those who transfer this to their relatives, friends, acquaintances and colleagues.

Although we live in an age of information where everything evolves very fast, we still have the power to control our thoughts and feelings. If you have read the book carefully and done all the exercises, you must have reached the conclusion that nobody can tell you anymore what beliefs you should have about certain things and about your capabilities. You are the one who adds significance to the events that happened in your life.

Success leaves it mark. Remember that. You might be among those who read piles of books on how to succeed in your life, who attend numerous seminars and buy all the tapes, which are available about personal growth and success, but you still have not succeeded. Perhaps you were just one-step away from success, from setting a sales record, from creating loving relationship--but nothing happened. Why? I will share that with you in a minute.

To be successful and wealthy does not mean only to work hard and have a lot of money. To be successful and wealthy is not only a matter of marketing and sales. It is not only capability and talent that matter. I know a lot of people, who are very capable, talented and smart, but they have financial problems all the time, or they are dissatisfied. I know many who are very rich and successful but not contented.

To be successful, wealthy and contented also means to think in a specific way. It also means to have a specific way of looking at everything that happens around us and at what we yearn for in our lives. It means a specific perspective on the things that happen to us. To acknowledge that what revolves around you it is not as important as the meaning we give to what happens to ourselves. To simplify: everything that happens within you is far more important than what is going on around you. It is very important how you handle your feelings that control the whole wheel of life. It is important that you are able to handle your fears and limiting beliefs, which can ruin even the biggest garden of capabilities and talents.

I am sure that you have found in this book much useful information that can change your life and help you to achieve happiness, satisfaction, wealth, improved health and feelings and the optimum level of motivation. However, you have to be aware that information without action is like a car without gas. With the help of the book, audio programs and seminars, you will learn how to put things into your life, and not only to dream about doing so. The only thing which has power today is action, which brings us closer to the set goals and fulfilled dreams.

I do not know how you obtained this book, but I do know that it came to you with a certain intention. If it was given as a gift, one day you might find out that this was the biggest gift in your life. It is up to you what you do with it. The book you are holding in your hands can be an excellent tool for the start of a new day; you can use it to relax yourself or for motivation or inspiration when you are going through hard times; the book can be an outstanding gift for your friends, children or coworkers, which

THE CONCLUSION

can be given on various occasions or simply when you would like to send somebody the message that you love him (her), and that you do care.

I like to give books because I am aware that a book can change somebody's view of life, as it did for me. The book can be your best friend, your tutor and teacher, and especially when you would like to tell somebody something, but he will not listen to you, or you cannot say it directly. Of course, this is not going to be the last book you ever read. I would like to encourage you to a lifetime of learning and progress. Only in this way will you be able to keep lasting happiness and contentment.

I cannot promise you that because of this book you will become the most successful person in the world. I cannot promise you that you are going to be the happiest person on earth. I do not make this kind of promise. But I can assure you that by using the instructions and strategies in this book you will become wealthier, more successful, healthier and happier than you ever dared dream. I can assure you that because I have worked with many people who achieved enviable results in all areas of their lives. In addition, I have another reason for my reassurance: I receive daily letters from participants of the seminar who have achieved in a short period of time, important results. Some of their responses can be read on our website.

When you decided to invest time and money in this book, you must have wanted something. I believe that you have received ideas and information with which you can direct your ship of success to the open sea of opportunity, love and fulfillment. Until our ships meet somewhere on the open sea or in port, I wish you much love, happiness and contentment. I would be glad if you could read your own story of success in the next book. I will be glad for any letter that you send me, each one where I read how you were able, with the ideas from this book to change your life for the better. I do read each letter personally, and keep them in a drawer. It was an honor to be in your company while you were reading the book. Although we have not yet met, I have to tell you that I love you, and that I am glad I could share my experiences with you.

I am sure that we connected on the way. I am sure that we will keep in touch. You can write to me about how the ideas helped you to improve your life; you can attend one of my seminars. Listen to audio programs. Considering that, the world is small; there is a strong possibility that we will meet somewhere coincidentally. You can grab my sleeve. I would be glad if you could share your life story with me. Each of us has a wonderful and at the same time important life story, in which he is the main actor. When you write the story of your success, remember that sometimes we have to adopt changes and make changes in the script. Be flexible and ready for change, and in that way, you will surely be successful and contented.

A lot of love, happiness and contentment are in my wishes for you and please know that:

> "Everyone has a fair turn to be as great as he pleases."
> - Jeremy Collier

With Love

Yours Smiljan Mori

ABOUT THE AUTHOR

SMILJAN MORI, BUSINESS AND LIFE COACH FOR SUCCESS

Smiljan provides a model which inspires thousands of people on how to live a happy, contented and successful life!

If you are wondering who Smiljan Mori is, he's a joyful and decisive man, who every day breaks-down the stereotypes of the serious nature of life's problems. He is living proof of his story, which clearly shows that we can all be princes and princesses in our own fairy tale. We just have to wish for it strongly enough.

Born in 1972, Smiljan Mori spent his early years in Vurmat, along the river Drava. After finishing secondary cadet school, where he graduated as the top cadet of his class (at Police Cadet School), he continued his studies at the Police College where he was also top student. Later, at the Faculty of Law, he was among the top graduates. Smiljan is an attorney by education, but has worked professionally in the field of sales, insurance operations and investments for the majority of his adult life.in and private life.

Smiljan is more than just a lecturer, he is a magician of events, where you are taken over by his leadership, charisma, amazing energy, and humor. He's a life coach and a visionary who teaches us how to look at life from different perspectives. Smiljan Mori educates, inspires and entertains by telling stories, and sharing his remarkable experience which allows people to put his knowledge into immediate practice.

Mori's seminars and events visited over 50 countries and more than 150,000 people in the last ten years. As a motivational leader, Smiljan Mori gave lectures in Slovenia, Russia, Belarus, Kazakhstan, and Ukraine, where his events were attended by thousands. In one public appearance in St. Petersburg, Russia, 12,000 people attended. In Slovenia alone together with M.Sc. Aleš Lisac, he reached a record attendance in filling an auditorium with more than 4,000 people.

With his motivational trainings, counseling and organizational seminars such as *Wake Up The Fire In You, Wake Up The Millionaire In You, Become A Winner, Perfect Life, Anything Is Possible*, Smiljan Mori has helped many entrepreneurs reach success and excellence. With his work, Mr. Mori inspires top female and male managers and directors of businesses by clearly pointing a path for achieving excellence, as well as, personal growth. He has endurance-strengthened Olympic athletes, worked with the female ski A-team from Slovenia and with football players, four of which were at the World Cup in Africa.

As a visiting lecturer, Mr. Mori inspires students and pupils at schools everywhere. With his revolutionary seminar, *Emotional Sales*, Smiljan has taught thousands of salesmen and their supervisors how to be better producing salesmen.

Smiljan Mori is the founder and director of two successful companies. In 1997, he founded Insurance Agency Mori, his first

ABOUT THE SMILJAN MORI COMPANIES

company. It has been recognized as one of the finest in Central Eastern Europe. Together with his co-workers, Mr. Mori provided for financial security and built a foundation of financial solidity for more than 60,000 Slovenian families and entrepreneurs.

In 2000, he established the company Success Systems, d. o. o., and with his techniques and methods for permanent change and progress, Smiljan has helped thousands of people around the world change their lives for the better.

He is a recognized writer, author of the best-seller *MotivAction for Life*, the booklet *Mini Motivator*, the books Me, d.o.o., and *Zigzag Formula of Success*. He also authored numerous scientific and popular articles, and the audio programs Think Like Winners and With Motivation to Succeed, which is recognized as the first audio program for motivation and personal development in Slovenia, and the program *Lose Weight Healthfully, Eat Smart*.

Mr. Mori is the author of a unique procedure for protection of entrepreneurs and families which are the basis for his bestseller *Foundation of Financial Independence*, and *The Best Business in the World*. In addition, he co-authored one of the bestsellers in the United States of America, *Wake Up and Live The Life You Love*, with recognized authors Marc Victor Hansen, Wayne Dyer, Robert Allen and others.

Smiljan is a member of the elite association of professional financial advisors Million Dollar Round Table and Top of the Table. He is engaged in several international, transnational, and intercontinental networks of motivators, leaders, coaches and authors that inspire people to create success in their lives.

Smiljan believes that success occurs first in our head. Surely, you must have heard the saying: IT IS ALL IN YOUR HEAD. It's true! However, has anyone ever showed you that? With Smiljan, you learn once and for all the meaning of the saying. In the last seven years, he studied the latest findings of Neuroscience in the field of success, motivation and management.

These findings are now available under the brand-name NEUROSUCCESS™ and THE WORK MOTIVACTION™, where you can discover how to become the designer of your own destiny.

ABOUT THE SMILJAN MORI COMPANIES

ALL YOU HAVE TO KNOW ABOUT FINANCES IN THE 21ST CENTURY

At last! Revealed "the secrets" of insurance, banking and other financial institutions, which you might overlook in the great number of offers on which your "pile" of money will depend!

Agencija Mori d.o.o.	life insurance
Partizanska cesta 6	accidental insurance
2000 Maribor	rent insurance
tel: 02/23 48 400	real estate insurance
fax:02/23 48 405	car insurance
	mutual fund
	...and much, much more....

email: smiljan.mori@smiljanmori.com

ABOUT THE SMILJAN MORI PROGRAMMES

- MotivAction Intelligence™
- S.E.A.R.C.H. Model Lifestyle™
- MotivAction Intelligence Coaching™
- Flourishing Thinking™
- MQ™

Smiljan Mori is an internationally renowned author, speaker, coach, and consultant. He shows individuals and organizations the unexpected keys to cultivate their MotivAction Intelligence (MQ); the ultimate leverage point for creating S.E.A.R.C.H. Model Lifestyle (Sell More, Earn More, Relax More, Connect More, More Happiness and Free Time).

Smiljan is a gifted speaker whether he's engaged in small intimate groups, or if he is the master presenter in front of large groups of tens of thousands. He is passionate about helping individuals, organizations and businesses to deepen their understanding of Flourishing Thinking and to help them create results that are vital to them.

In addition to speaking in front of large audiences, leading selected corporate programs, conducting life-transformational events and retreats, and working with a handful of coaching clients, Smiljan also runs workshops for business leaders, trainers, coaches, and consultants.

Smiljan Mori is dedicated to providing the highest quality of MotivAction Intelligence and Flourishing Thinking training, coaching and consulting services, in the form of professional development and corporate programs.

Corporate programs

MotivAction Intelligence Coaching

Neuroscience, Positive Psychology and NLP coaching, to unlock potential and resources in your employees, sales people, executive managers and business.

Is your organization struggling with:

Low morale?
Overwhelmed employees?
Loss of top performers?
Ineffective leadership?
Unmet performance goals?
Low Productivity?
Lack of Team Work?

MotivAction Intelligence coaching helps professional staff align their values with those of the entire organization. "In my fifteen years of experience, I have found that when you strengthen a professional's inner traits, in addition to developing their outer skills, the entire organization benefits. Your best employees stay and thrive, your company goals are met, and inspiration replaces complacency.

Areas where an understanding of Flourishing Thinking is particularly relevant and have a strong impact include:

ABOUT THE SMILJAN MORI PROGRAMS

Leadership, Team Building, Strategy and Vision, Performance Enhancement, Resilience, Gratitude, Courage, Creativity and Innovation, Decision Making, Listening and Communication, Persuasion and Influence, Dealing with Conflicts, Culture Change, Problem Solving, and Coaching Skills.

Life Transformation and Flourishing Coaching, Retreats and Intensives

The MotivAction Intelligence Coaching

The MotivAction Intelligence Coaching Program takes place over the course of one year and includes the following elements:

Preparatory materials
An MQ 1:1 Intensive (3 days, in person)
A monthly, 2-hour MQ Coaching session
Spot-check phone and email support
VIP access to selected events & retreats

The MotivAction Intelligence and Flourishing 1:1 Retreat

- you and Smiljan spend 7 days in person doing 1:1 Coaching and mentoring
- including all of the benefits of Smiljan's MotivAction Intelligence Coaching Program

The MotivAction Intelligence Retreat

- you spend 5 days with Smiljan Mori and a small group of 15-20 people

The MotivAction Intelligence 1:1 Intensive

- we spend 3 days doing 1:1 coaching and mentoring, 2-3 sessions per day
- you also get 3 follow up coaching calls

For other corporate-speaking engagements, keynote speeches, trainings, and seminars go to www.SmiljanMori.com. You can connect with Smiljan using the following methods:

Twitter
Linkedin
Email: smiljan.mori@smiljanmori.com
Website: www.SmiljanMori.com
Phone: 00386 30 671 073
Address:
Smiljan Mori Success Systems, d.o.o.
Partizanska cesta 6
2000 Maribor
Slovenia

To get more success tools and templates to take your life or business to the next level check www.smiljanmori.com

You will receive templates for:

The Habit Clarifier™
The Old Habit Destroyer™
The New Habit Builder™
The Next Level Action™

ABOUT THE SMILJAN MORI PROGRAMS

THE PYRAMID OF SUCCESS

Everything is Possible
> Motivation Seminars
> Seminars About How To Deal With Money
> Sales Seminars
> Seminars About Leadership
> Pyramid Of Success

Perfect Life Time Management Motivation Day

Become a Winner Rhetoric -
> How To Talk In Front Of The Public
> Communication in Business
> ...and much , much more...

> "Achieve in one year more than the majority do in their whole lives."

Seminars for managers, executive managers, private enterprises and top salesmen.

www.SmiljanMori.com

Through the Smiljan Mori audio program "With The Motivation To Succeed!" you will discover how to add a new and deeper meaning to your life. Smiljan will show you how to live the life you want and deserve.

You will learn how to motivate yourself instantly for top achievements, find and develop your strategy of success, deal with emotions, destroy old patterns and self-limiting beliefs with anchoring, and much, much more...

45 MINUTES OF MOTIVATION FOR TOP ACHIEVEMENTS

The treasury of wisdom is the booklet of inspirational thoughts and proverbs of Smiljan Mori.

> "Be careful that the disease of failure doesn't infect those remaining healthy cells of hope, which could grow into a story of success."
> Smiljan Mori

Did you ever have the feeling that you are stuck in your personal and professional life? This booklet may be just the thing you need; the motivational messages it contains will redirect you to the right track!

RECOMMENDED READING

KIM H. SANG: 1001 Ways to Motivate Yourself and Others (U.S.A., Wethersfield: Turtle Press, 1996).

MARC VICTOR HANSEN in JOE BATTEN: Mojster motiviranja (Bled: Vernar consulting, d.o.o., 1998).

ROBERT T. KIYOSAKI: Rich Kid Smart Kid (U.S.A., New York: Warner Books, 2001).

ROBERT T. KIYOSAKI: Bogati o~ka, revni o~ka (Ljubljana: Lisac & Lisac, 2001).

NIKOLA GRUBI[A, BORIS VENE: Iz dnevnika milijonarja ... ali bogastvo je v nas (Bled: Phantom, 2001).

NAPOLEON HILL: Z idejo do bogastva (Amalietti, 1999).

ZIG ZIGLAR: Vidimo se na vrhu (Ljubljana: Lisac & Lisac, 1999).

RICHARD BANDLER and JOHN GRINDER: Patterns of the Hypnotic Techniques of Milton H. Erickson, M.D. Volume 1 (U.S.A., California: Meta Publications, 1975).

JOHN GRINDER, JUDITH DeLOZIER and RICHARD BANDLER: Patterns of the Hypnotic Techniques of Milton H. Erickson, M.D. Volume 2 (U.S.A., California: Meta Publications, 1977).

SIDNEY C. WALKER: Trusting YourSelf (U.S.A., Colorado: High Plains Publishing Co., 1988).

ROBERT B. CIALDINI: Influence (U.S.A., New York: William Morrow and Company, Inc., 1993).

MARGARET P. KORB, JEFFREY GORRELL and VERNON VAN DE RIET: Gestalt therapy (U.S.A., Upper Saddle River: A Pearson Education Company, 1989).

ROBERT B. DILTS: Modeling With NLP (U.S.A., California: Meta Publications, 1998).

RICHARD BANDLER: Time for a Change (U.S.A., California: Meta Publications, 1993).

ROBERT B. DILTS: Changing Belief Systems with NLP (U.S.A., California: Meta Publications, 1990).

DENNIS GREENBERGER, CHRISTINE A. PADESKY: Mind over mood (U.S.A., New York: The Guilford Press, 1995).

JOHN J. EMERICK Jr.: Be the Person You Want to Be (U.S.A., California: Prima Publishing, 1997).

HERBERT BENSON, M.D.: Timeless Healing (U.S.A., New York: Fireside, 1996).

ROBERT DILTS, TIM HALLBOM & SUZI SMITH: Beliefs (U.S.A., Oregon: Metamorphous Press, 1990).

VIKTOR E. FRANKL.: Man's Search for Meaning (U.S.A., Massachusetts: Beacon Press, 1992).

JOSEPH MURPHY: The Power of Your Subconscious Mind (U.S.A., New York: Bantam Books, 2000).

VIKTOR E. FRANKL, M.D.: The Doctor and the Soul (U.S.A., New York: Vintage Books, 1986).

VIKTOR E. FRANKL: The Will to Meaning (U.S.A., New York: Meridian, 1988).

NORMAN COUSINS: Anatomy of an illness (U.S.A., New York: Bantam Books, 1979).

DAVID D. BURNS: Feeling Good (U.S.A., New York: Avon books, 1999).

CLAUDE M. BRISTOL: The Magic of Believing (U.S.A., New York: Pocket books, 1969).

THOMAS CLEARY: The Art of Wealth (U.S.A., Florida: Health Communications, 1998).

ALLAN & BARBARA PEASE: Why Men Don't Listen & Women Can't Read Maps (Pease International, 2001).

W. MITCHELL: It's Not What Happens to You, It's What You Do About It (U.S.A., Arvada: Phoenix Press, 2001).

JACK WELCH: Jack (Great Britain, London: Headline Book Publishing, 2001).

WALLACE D. WATTLES & Dr. JUDITH POWELL: The Science of Getting Rich (U.S.A., Florida: Top of the Mountain Publishing, 2002).

JOHN ROGER and PETER McWILLIAMS: You Can't Afford the Luxury of a Negative Thought (Great Britain, London: Thorsons, 1991).

DAWN CALLAN: Awakening The Warrior Within (U.S.A., California: Tenacity Press, 1999).

LEE CARROLL and JAN TOBER: The Indigo Children (U.S.A., California: Hay House, 1999).

DEEPAK CHOPRA: The Way of the Wizard (U.S.A., New York: Harmony Books, 1995).

JOHN C. MAXWELL: Success (U.S.A., Tennessee: J. Countryman, 2000).

DEEPAK CHOPRA: The Deeper Wound (U.S.A., New York: Harmony Books, 2001).

HARRY S. DENT: The Great Boom Ahead (U.S.A., New York: Hyperion, 1993).

CHARLES E. MELLON: Winning Wealth Strategies (U.S.A., Nevada: Sierra Newport Publishing, 2001).

CHARLES R. SCHWAB: You're Fifty – Now What? (U.S.A., Crown Business, 2001).

GARY MOORE: Spiritual Investments (U.S.A., Pennsylvania: Templeton Foundation Press, 1998).

CHARLES B. CARLSON: Eight Steps to Seven Figures (U.S.A., New York: Acurrency Book, 2000).

STEPHEN M. POLLAN: Kon~ajte v bankrotu (Ljubljana: Orbis, 1998).

JOHN ROBBINS: Diet for a New America (U.S.A., California: H J Kramer Book, 1987).

JOHN ROBBINS: The Food Revolution (U.S.A., California: Conari Press, 2001).

STU MITTLEMAN: Slow Burn (U.S.A., New York, Harper Collins, 2000).

BARBARA HOBERMAN LEVINE: Your Body Believes Every Word You Say (U.S.A., Connecticut, WordsWork Press, 2000).

CONNIRAE ANDREAS, STEVE ANDREAS: Heart of the Mind (U.S.A., Utah: Real People Press, 1989).

CANDACE B. PERT: Molecules of Emotion (U.S.A., New York: Simon & Schuster, 1999).

TAG POWELL & JUDITH POWELL: Silva Mind Mastery for the '90s (U.S.A, Florida: Top Of The Mountain Publishing, 1996).

NORMAN COUSINS: Head First (U.S.A., New York: Penguin Books, 1990).

JOSE SILVA: The Silva Mind Control Method (U.S.A., New York: Pocket Books, 1978).

FRANK CAPRIO and JOSEPH R. BERGER: Healing Yourself with Self–Hypnosis (U.S.A., New Jersey: Prentice Hall, 1998).

ANTHONY ROBBINS: Awaken The Giant Within (U.S.A., New York: Fireside, 1997).

ANTHONY ROBBINS: Prebudite velikana v sebi (Ljubljana: Lisac & Lisac, 2000).

KEVIN HOGAN: Tinnitus: Turning The Volume Down (U.S.A., Eagan: Network 3000 Publishing, 1998).

If you want more information about my seminars, keynotes, trainings you can visit (www.smiljanmori.com) and download a full catalog!

www.ingramcontent.com/pod-product-compliance
Lightning Source LLC
LaVergne TN
LVHW051822080426
835512LV00018B/2691